FLOWERS BY DESIGN

Creating Arrangements for Your Space

—

INGRID CAROZZI

Creator of *Tin Can Studios*

ABRAMS, NEW YORK

for Stella

CONTENTS

INTRODUCTION

Flowers speak to us in a language that knows no borders. They move us and thrill us, evoke joy and sadness, and call our attention to the beauty that fills our world. Put a simple arrangement on the table and watch your home come alive.

We know how happy flowers can make us, and I for one was not a bit surprised to learn that this had actually been scientifically proven*—the act of giving flowers, as it turns out, stimulates the production of the feel-good hormone oxytocin, while receiving them triggers the release of dopamine.

As the natural wonders they are, flowers are truly transformative. Just looking at flowers, touching them, or watching them grow increases our sense of well-being—and receiving them makes us feel appreciated and loved. I don't think I had fully come to appreciate the power of flowers before my first book, *Handpicked*, was published a few years ago and I started hearing from people from all over the globe. I was moved to learn that my story and what I do had inspired people, young and old, to take up the trade, some even on a professional level, and to pursue this as a new hobby.

The thought that something I do here in Brooklyn can influence someone an ocean or two away is hard for me to wrap my head around sometimes. But the proof comes when a student at a workshop brings in a copy of my book that they bought from Amazon Mexico and then asks me to sign it, or when someone texts me a picture of my book cover from an independent bookstore in Australia, Germany, England, or Sweden. I still get these sweet messages every week! Having lived in six different countries, it feels pretty special to be connected to the world in this way, through my love for flowers.

For me, flowers have always been about people and the way they bring us together. So when I was asked to come up with some ideas for a follow-up to my book, I didn't have to think that hard or for that long.

I wanted to showcase my work and the way I feel about flowers, what I know they can offer to each of us. I drew on the people in my life for inspiration, as well as their own relationships to flowers. And I'm excited to share all the insights and knowledge I was able to gather here. Writing a book is such an incredible honor, and I hope each one of you who reads this book will get a sense of who I am and what I do, and that my love of flowers will become yours as well.

* "Why Flowers Make Us Happy," Loretta G. Breuning, PhD, *Psychology Today*, Jan 21, 2017.

HOW I GOT HERE

I get questions about my work all the time, and the most common of them is: How do you become a florist?

For me, it was a little bit of chance that brought me into the floral design business. Before getting my degree from Parsons School of Design, I worked as an event planner for The Swedish-American Chamber of Commerce in New York. When my former boss called me up years later to ask me to come up with a floral concept for an event for them, I was surprised, to say the least. It was a black-tie affair called "From Farm to Fork," where growers, chefs, and food purveyors were invited to share their philosophies on food and sustainability.

I had no previous experience with flowers, but as a designer I knew how to develop a concept, and my former boss was convinced I was the right person for the job, so I accepted the challenge.

My thoughts went immediately to what brought all these people together: fresh produce and sustainability. I have always loved to cook, and working with flowers was in many ways similar to putting a meal together. In both pursuits, you do everything you can to source the best, preferably local and seasonal, ingredients; you spend time and attention on your prep work and execution; and once you put everything together you present the results and hope that the person sharing your meal or receiving your flower arrangement is blown away. My favorite food editor Sam Sifton once wrote: "There is great pleasure to be had in cooking for others," and I feel the same way about working with flowers. To me, a thoughtfully composed arrangement gets its soul once it is shared with another person.

The result was flower boxes I built myself from salvaged wood and filled with artichokes, crown dill, decorative cabbages, berries, and fresh flowers. I took a chance, and it worked out. The event was successful, and the reactions to my arrangements were so strong that I started to think that this might be something I was good at.

Floristry is hard work. On a daily basis I spend more time washing out buckets and schlepping stuff from place to place in taxis and trucks than arranging flowers. Building a successful business often means spending hours on the phone with clients, explaining pricing and logistics and discussing design. A lot of my time is also spent recruiting new talent, training them, and motivating a team. A pretty small part of my workweek, I would say no more than twenty percent, is actually spent arranging flowers. But at the end of the day, I wouldn't have it any other way.

As much as I love what I do, solely the love of flowers is not enough. I regularly find myself at the flower market when they open, at five thirty A.M., and it is still

dark outside. And if I had an event the night before, I may not have had more than couple of hours to sleep.

So if you dream of becoming a florist, as many of you do, my advice would be to educate yourself first. Take some classes. There are a number of great flower schools out there—in fact, I have taken courses and teach at a few of them—and I cannot emphasize enough how important it is to learn how to condition and care for the flowers you are going to work with. Get an internship with a well-established florist in your area where you can see the less glamorous side of floristry. Take some workshops with your favorite florists. There are so many wonderful and talented floral designers out there who, just like me, love to teach. So see for yourself how you like the actual work.

There are so many designers in the field these days, but few actually know flower care. Buying and arranging flowers for yourself is one thing; handling commercial accounts is another altogether. You can make the most beautiful flower arrangements in the world, but in order to be successful (and keep your clients!), you have to keep your flowers healthy and alive.

In the back of this book I list a few schools I have personal knowledge about, where you can learn the basics of sustainable floristry and build a foundation to stand on.

UPS AND DOWNS AND UPS

A lot has happened since I started my company back in 2013. My business has grown from a one-woman operation in a shed behind a warehouse, where I built a makeshift cooler with a portable AC unit and a drop cloth, to the internationally recognized floral design firm I am proud to run today.

In the years I have been in business, I have grown out of one space after another, I have seen my first book successfully launch in several countries, and I have had the honor of working with the most amazing clients at some spectacular venues. My style as a florist has also evolved since my last book, which I hope will be evident from these pages.

When I set out to write this book, I wanted to take you on a journey—a journey where not every single picture matched the others like they do in a perfect Instagram feed. Uniformity gets old pretty fast, and in a way, so do trends.

I want my designs to reflect the time we live in, but at the same time be timeless. Good design always looks right and never goes out of style, and, as I have learned, a good business is a flexible business that can, when needed, pivot on a penny.

For the first six years, I worked out of an old warehouse in Red Hook, Brooklyn. It was just a five-minute bike ride from where I lived then and really convenient. I shared the space with a group of artists and craftspeople and there were tons of things going on at any given time. That's where Tin Can Studios came to be, and I loved it there.

But as my business grew I needed more space. Since we recycle and reuse as much as we can, there were vases, pots, and urns stacked from floor to ceiling. The storage rooms were overflowing with everything needed to make a variety of arrangements and installations. Before major events, there could be fifteen florists and assistants literally tripping over each other, and my walk-in cooler would be stuffed to its breaking point.

So I started looking around. On the other side of Brooklyn, I thought I had found a perfect spot: a sprawling event space located right where East Williamsburg and Bushwick intersect. Not only was this place amazing, in an empty part of the lot, I was offered the opportunity to design my own studio from stacked shipping containers, complete with floor-to-ceiling windows and a rooftop garden and greenhouse. The vastly increased space would also allow me to host more of my own workshops, something I really enjoy and want to spend more time doing.

Then the pandemic struck, and everything changed overnight. We were on our way to the Frick's Young Fellows Ball and a behind-the-scenes photo shoot for this book, with a truck full of flowers, when we found out that all events were now "on pause." This meant there would be no event work for me or my staff for the foreseeable future.

After absorbing the initial shock, I realized I would have to reinvent myself and figure out a way to quickly take my business in a new direction. I honestly didn't feel that motivated. I had already spent seven years hustling and building something out of nothing, but I reminded myself why I started this business: to support my daughter and to be able to stay in New York so she could be close to her dad. Then I thought about why I loved working with flowers in the first place.

For me, it had always been about bringing that special excitement and joy to people through flowers, and now I would need to come up with a new, safe way of doing that. And like so many others, I would have to do that from home, at least for a while.

My newest venture, Bloom Box—where customers get a box of curated flowers shipped to their front door and then get to arrange them with me via video—was born quickly thereafter, right on my kitchen table.

As much as I missed doing big events with my crew, this new line of work, where I get to connect with so many people over flowers in such a personal and intimate way, has genuinely brought me such unexpected happiness.

In this book, I show you a few examples of the amazing arrangements my customers have made in their own homes, and the techniques I show are applicable to whatever blooms you have at hand—straight from the supermarket or picked in your own backyard. It is all about having fun and creating beauty and bringing nature into our homes in a relaxed way, all while focusing on enjoying the process.

WHAT I DO AND HOW I DO IT

As a person who "just" works with flowers, I have had to learn how to solder, use power tools, cut glass, and drive a box truck, to name a few skills acquired during my career. It is challenging work, but it is also very inspiring.

As a floral designer, no two days are ever alike and each day can bring a new set of challenges. Over the past few years, for example, I have been asked by my clients to create large floral installations, using sustainable methods, that must last for ten days, as well as giant flower backdrops for awards ceremonies. I have built flower arrangements inside blocks of ice when asked to come up with a cool concept for a cutting-edge museum gala.

At Tin Can Studios, we do a lot of events—small and large, corporate and private—and our goal is always the same: to exceed all expectations, make dreams come true, and leave our client breathless. Though no two occasions are ever alike, my involvement usually begins when a client contacts us for an upcoming event. It can be for a runway fashion show, a window display, a wedding, or an art fair—anything in which flowers can convey a message or set the tone.

And so no two arrangements are exactly alike and they are not supposed to be. Faced with a new project, I usually start by developing a concept and a color palette. I try to understand what kind of message my client wants to convey with the flowers. What are they trying to say?

Sometimes, a painting is all I need to guide me. For another event, I might look at architecture, or pick up the September issue of *Vogue*, just to get a sense of what is happening right now in other fields.

In my head, I am also going through what flowers are in season and where to source them. At the studio, we never use recipes. Instead we talk about width and height of each arrangement, and style and stem count. This functions more as a rough guide for our designs. It is a more painterly way of working and my freelancers find it more inspiring to work this way, and I believe you will as well!

To create arrangements in Tin Can Studios' distinctive style, we frequently use keywords, like *asymmetry*, *up and down movement*, *gesture*, *contrast*, *height variation*, *negative space*, *moments*, and *texture*—these fly around the studio when we prepare for our events.

Take The Winter Show, a premier design fair held yearly at the historic Park Avenue Armory. I have worked with them for four consecutive years, and each time has offered me a unique opportunity to challenge myself; to dig deep, think big, widen my perspective, and in the end, really create a lot of buzz.

Historically, the flower arrangements at The Winter Show were traditional— but I was contacted as the designers and organizers wanted to emphasize that collecting antiques caters to a younger generation as well. They wanted this to be evident and really come across in the flower arrangements.

I thought about the space—literally an entire block—and the ideas I needed to convey. I also wanted the flowers to be pretty edgy and the shapes untraditional. We used a de Gournay wallpaper with images from Le Jardin Secret in Marrakesh as our main inspiration for the mood board and they loved it.

The days leading up to an event like that are busy and chaotic and exciting and fun. Thousands of individual flowers have to be sourced, conditioned, arranged, and prepared for delivery; structures for large-scale installations built, trucks rented, and delivery people hired.

Everything has to be kept fresh for days, at times up to ten, which often takes a lot of planning. You also have to stick to their budget, and the bigger the budget, the more you risk losing. On the day of the event, you need to have a thorough plan and all your bases covered. And since The Winter Show is held in January, you hope that it won't snow and that the temperatures won't be below freezing as you load and unload your flowers.

At the end of the day, you cannot control everything, so have a plan but keep the process organic and adopt a flexible approach. Events like these are rewarding, from a professional perspective. Doing what I love on such a large scale is truly a special experience.

WHAT I KNOW

Giving and sharing was a big part of both my business philosophy and marketing strategy from the get-go. Instead of throwing out my flower arrangements after each event, I brought them back to my studio; from there I distributed them, often on bicycle, to cafés, restaurants, and small businesses in the area. It broke my heart to see the flowers go in the garbage can when I could just make a few phone calls and find new homes for them.

Since then, our efforts to minimize waste and spread joy have taken on new and inspiring shapes and forms. Tin Can Studios has happily partnered with a number of local initiatives. One of them is BloomAgainBklyn, a wonderful charity organization that collects leftover flowers, which are then donated to nursing homes, hospitals, and schools. My aim is to give my flowers a second life and, in the process, make my neighbors, and those who seldom get flowers, happy.

Teaching is another direction, though not exactly a new one, that my flowers have taken me. In my twenties, while still living in Sweden, I taught Swedish, English, and math as a special resource teacher. It was really hard work, and I often felt so bad for the struggles these kids had to go through. But in the end, watching them learn and grow was truly rewarding.

In the past few years, I have shared my knowledge of flowers with groups of students at FlowerSchool New York, where I have taught sustainable methods and how to create large-scale installations such as floral chandeliers, runways, and walls. I have also hosted my own workshops and taught at The New York Botanical Garden. At the studio, we have trained countless interns and apprentices. Many of them now work for me as freelancers, while others have gone on to start their own businesses. In addition, I offer online, virtual classes for hobby florists as well as workshops for corporate clients.

Through FlowerSchool New York, I also had the pleasure and honor of teaching an international master class in Casa Azul—the former home of Frida Kahlo and her husband Diego Rivera, now a museum—in Mexico City. This was an incredible opportunnity and moment for me, both professionally and personally.

Teaching not only allows me to share what I know and love, it also gives me a chance to explore and experiment with new techniques.

GOING BEYOND
TO FIND INSPIRATION

When I started out as a florist, social media had not evolved to what it is today, although it was certainly a go-to source for inspiration. Instagram and Pinterest certainly have had—and still have—enormous influence on us and on the creative process, but I find myself more often seeking out primary sources. I make a real effort to find inspiration elsewhere by studying trends in fashion, interior design, cinema, theater, and art exhibits firsthand. I also find a lot of inspiration in food.

Books have always been a passion of mine, and a true inspiration. Though I mostly adhere to a minimalistic style at home, I am a bit of a "bookaholic." I recently had to rent a storage unit to hold my substantial collection of design and flower books.

One book that I really love, and can even relate to on a certain level, is *The Surprising Life of Constance Spry*, the London florist who, in the early part of the last century, made a name for herself in the male-dominated field of floral design. She foraged her flowers, just like I grew up doing in Sweden, and made what were then considered rule-breaking arrangements. Instead of traditional arrangements, based on symmetry, she created her own set of rules. But in the end, she broke those too and decided to create what she liked, based on what she had at hand. She was not only brave and brilliant but ahead of her time.

ALL ABOUT PEOPLE

It's people that inspire me every day, people that inform my work; Whether it's someone I have worked with or someone I would love to work with; people I know and love and people I have never met but admire from a distance. So I looked again to people for this book, and it wasn't hard to find the right ones—editing my list down to fewer than a dozen people was the tough part.

The talented men and women in this book are not only successful in their respective fields, they also love flowers and have precise ideas about them. Like Kate, who is inspired by them every day in her artistry; or Audrey, who turns leftover flowers that would have otherwise gone to waste into the most beautiful fabric dyes; or Fredrik, who serves them up as ingredients in culinary compositions.

I like to think that Tin Can Studios, my floral design company, was born where people and flowers intersect and launched from my love for both. And I worked to capture that fruitful relationship here.

In this book, I wanted to broaden my scope to feature other artists and professionals, and how flowers relate to their lives and work. Each Tastemaker was chosen for their aesthetic, personality, and profession, and I feel that they offer a wide representation of how flowers can and do impact our lives. I worked with each of them to create arrangements inspired by their tastes and based off of mood boards I created to reflect their unique styles. Each arrangement was designed to reflect the unlimited potential and possibility that's available when working with flowers—there's an arrangement or inspiration here for every taste, to fit any space, for any occasion.

TASTEMAKERS

Audrey Louise Reynolds

ARTISANAL DYE MAKER

My connection to flowers is hard to explain; it is much bigger than me. It has always been there, like a language I never had to learn.

I've been growing flowers since babyhood, alongside my great-grandmother, grandmother, and mother, and I am more comfortable covered in dirt than clean. I am a gardener, and playing with flowers has offered me an escape. I feel so grateful that my need to touch and manipulate these plants has allowed me to support myself while making a positive environmental impact.

Doing what I do is not a choice but a means of survival from some of my life traumas. Color therapy has been my therapy. Flowers are magic, full of vitamins and beneficial properties, while aesthetically pleasing.

In my work I was originally using the obvious color that a flower is. Grabbing it at its fullest potential and stopping that color as a moment in time. I could say this pink existed as a living thing on this day, at this time, and here it was, preserved for us to appreciate. Now I have gone deeper, manipulating nature into unlocking all sorts of colors, never losing appreciation for where we started, but also seeing what sort of journey we could go on together. It is science, it is curiosity, but mostly it's how I know to survive. —AUDREY

To bring some colors to their fullest potential, Audrey uses heat. To illustrate this step of the process, we gathered all the flowers we had used and stuck them in a dye pot.

Audrey and I were introduced to each other through our mutual interest in flowers—more precisely, the dead and the wilted ones I could no longer use but hated to throw away, which she wanted to make the natural fabric dyes she sells, some to the most high-end stores, like MoMa, Nike, and Roman and Williams.

There was something similar in the way we worked, using mostly our hands in the creative process. She also has the greatest respect for the planet, aiming for a close to zero footprint and no waste. Her studio was just a few blocks away from mine in Red Hook and I invited her over to discuss finding a way to repurpose my leftover flowers that would benefit both of us.

The ribbons she created with dyes derived from flowers—wilted petals and blooms that would otherwise have been discarded—were beautiful and unique; I used them for some very lucky brides. My flowers had gone full circle, from one wedding to next, and since the colors of the ribbons came from the flowers themselves, they always complemented each other.

Audrey has since moved away and now lives and works in upstate New York, so she can't come by for my leftovers anymore, but when I started making a list of potential tastemakers for my book, she immediately came to mind.

As an artist and entrepreneur, Audrey is one in a million. She combines her artistic talent with a good amount of business savvy, and her scientific knowledge just blows me away. There is a freedom to the way she approaches her work, but in order to set the perfect parameters for her dyes, she has to carefully examine both the fabric and its intended use, which is quite a process.

Her new place is amazing: an old farmhouse sitting on several acres of mostly wooded land, so foraging for greenery was a given. When I saw the photos Audrey sent me, my eye immediately went to an abandoned and overgrown flower garden adjacent to her new studio. The small space has an old wooden fence around it and a crooked gate: a perfect spot for hanging flowers to dry or setting a table for a small gathering using one of Audrey's hand-dyed cloths.

Audrey's dyes span the spectrum from vibrant to muted depending on their source—she uses everything from flower petals and algae to crushed and dried bones—but they are all rich and saturated, so I wanted the flower arrangements I created for her to reflect that. She had also told me about her grandmother's paintings, classic still lifes that had always inspired her and now cover her walls, so I looked to them for inspiration as well.

"Life is fragile, as is the color of a living thing. To harness that color at its fullest potential has become this endless game I can play with nature." —AUDREY

Wild and Loose Arrangement in a Footed Cast-Iron Vase

I wanted to make a really big arrangement to fill this outdoor space, but I didn't want it to look fussy or too precious; I wanted it to be more like Audrey Louise, a bit wild without being unorganized, and beautiful in a larger-than-life kind of way.

I made sure to bring a heavy cast-iron vase that wouldn't tip over in the wind. Since Audrey is all about conservation, I brought the leftover flowers I had in the studio: late fall peonies, a few different dahlias and ranunculus, and some roses and thistles. I knew there would be plenty of greenery for me to forage, but I wanted to incorporate some eucalyptus since she uses it in her dye making. We placed everything on top of a few of her hand-dyed linens.

WHAT I USED:

1 footed cast-iron vase with an approximate 8"-wide opening prepared with chicken wire as shown on page 133; 2 red star oncidium; 3–5 large deep red peonies; 4 mustard yellow garden roses; 3 pink garden roses; 6 orange tulips, 2 of them flexed as shown on page 115; 15–20 mixed ranunculus; 6 bicolored carnations; 5–7 purple lisianthus; 5 pink and blush spray roses; Eucalyptus and mixed foraged greenery and twigs, such as some blackberry or raspberry hybrid vines, toyon berry, pokeberry, and ninebark. On page 133, you can read more about how I approach large and loose arrangements like this.

Dahlias and Chrysanthemum on a String

Garlands can add such a beautiful accent or frame to any area. For Audrey's overgrown garden, I thought it would be fun to string some of my blooms that were clearly past their prime and could not have been used in other arrangements. Just using the heads, without their stems, made a strong impact. For a casual and effortless look, we cut all the garlands into different lengths.

WHAT I USED:

10 large dahlias or chrysanthemums per foot of garland; Fishing line; Embroidery needle; Sharp scissors

HOW I MADE IT:

The needle and fishing line easily penetrated the centers of the flowers and we did not need to knot the line to stop the flowers from sliding.

To finish the installation, we also hung bunches of lavender, thistle, strawflowers, and amaranthus on the fence to dry.

Hilary Robertson

STYLIST

Flowers make me happier; they are as essential to me as fresh air and good food. I spent my childhood playing in woods and gardens, creating imaginary homes for my dolls with twigs, leaves, branches, moss, and wildflowers. My village school was on the edge of woods, where a carpet of bluebells would appear every spring and playtime was spent collecting enormous bunches of them to take home to our mothers.

As an interior stylist, I often travel for work and I'm always thrilled to explore a new flower market. I especially like Brannan Street in San Francisco, where there's so much local foliage. Having flowers in every room in the house or even a hotel room acts as the best anti-depressant I know. —HILARY

"I sometimes find myself longing for a world of muted shades, where everything falls into a monochrome harmony, timeless and elegant." —INGRID

My work is all about texture and color and in order to create the vision my client wants, and has hired me to achieve, I often have to think big and go all out. After one of those colorful workweeks, I sometimes find myself longing for the world my friend Hilary inhabits: a world of muted shades of gray; a home where pinky taupe bedroom walls add color and everything falls into a monochrome restful harmony. And like this British transplant herself, the style is timeless and elegant.

A few years back, Hilary and I were both featured in a book called *Brooklyn Street Style,* and it was at the launch party for the book that we first met. Ever since then, we have wanted to do something together, and when I came up with this book idea, we finally got the chance.

I know Hilary is not "against" colors. As a stylist working all over the globe for clients like West Elm, Bloomingdale's, and *Vogue*, she is an expert in mixing and matching all kinds of colors and shades and getting it right. But since her home is as monochromatic as the ones she writes about in her book *Monochrome Home*, I wanted my flowers to reflect that.

Forgoing color, as a design choice, is surprisingly freeing. In a monochrome home, textures become more apparent while items of different periods and styles, and even patterns, blend nicely.

Hilary has exquisite taste and a precise eye. She can arrange the most random items into a pared-down and perfectly scaled still life. With my own Swedish-Italian esthetic, I really admire someone who has managed to cultivate a personal style based on restraint. Limiting colors and editing your palette down to a single shade and its hues takes discipline and effort.

As a backdrop, monochrome is often ideal, but as a concept for the flowers themselves, it is both challenging and exciting. It's a bit like taking photos in and black and white, focusing more on shape and impact. Most flowers come in color.

But some grasses come in more neutral hues, which would work well in this kind of environment, as would a muted ikebana, or a lush all-green arrangement.

The vases would also be simple, black and white. I always pay a lot of attention to my vases. The stackable ceramic vase from Bloomist felt new and unique in design; it would also be heavy enough to hold the large arrangement I had I mind. For my ikebana-inspired arrangement, Hilary lent me a perfect little bowl from OYOY Living Design.

As for the choice of flowers, Hilary is an omnivore, known to leave no blooms behind when she works on various photo shoots.

Hilary's brownstone apartment, set on a beautiful tree-lined street in historic Fort Greene, is by no means ascetic. It's rich in architectural detail and filled with beautiful, odd, and interesting things she and her husband have gathered during years of globetrotting and market hopping, things she loves to look at. Daylight streaming from floor-to-ceiling windows fills the rooms.

Ikebana-Inspired Arrangement
in a Ceramic Vase

I can't say enough about these simple but yet elegant arrangements that are becoming so popular. They fit just about anywhere and are really easy to make. You can use a variety of small bowls and vases.

For Hillary, it was also a natural choice since she is a minimalist and her marble mantel made for a perfect staging area.

WHAT I USED:

1 low ceramic vase with an approximate 5–6"-wide opening prepared with a flower frog as shown on page 125; 1 Oncostele Wildcat "Golden Red Star" orchid stem; 1 sea oats stem; 1 switchgrass stem; 1 black begonia leaf; 1 ornamental pepper "black pearl." See page 125 for more about how I approach ikebana-inspired arrangements.

Huge Green Arrangement in a
Stackable Ceramic Vase

This arrangement was perfect for the spot, and if you ever want to create something really large and powerful on a small budget, think green!

For this arrangement, I used a mix of foraged branches with some more eye-catching ones, like the chestnut branch that had fruits on it, but you can create an arrangement with similar impact using whatever grows nearby.

You will need to use a really heavy vase or weigh your vase down with rocks or stones.

WHAT I USED:

1 heavy ceramic vase with an approximate 7–8"-wide opening prepared with chicken wire as shown on page **133**; Tomatillo; Chestnut; Lemon verbena; Jasmine vine; Forsythia

Jade Purple Brown

ILLUSTRATOR

The natural beauty of flowers sparks joy in me whenever I stumble across them. Their lively colors, unique shapes, and exquisite textures inspire me to create. My work centers on strong contours, vibrant colors, and messages of optimism; a desire to create new, dynamic worlds of individuality and empowerment. Flowers weave through my pieces, inspiring viewers to create their own unique world in which they want to live, lifting their spirits along the way. —JADE

"Flowers make people happy and that's the emotion I want to evoke through my art." —JADE

I first came across Jade's work while working on color palettes for the MTV Staying Alive Foundation gala in 2018. I had been asked to create floral concepts using a mix of bold and vibrant colors, like teal, magenta, and yellow. Since I like finding references from other fields, I was overjoyed when I found Jade's fun and playful artwork. Her fearless, graphic style and amazing eye for color immediately drew me in. Instead of using my regular swatches for color matching, I just printed out a couple of her illustrations and walked over to the market.

I often think about the parallels between working with typography (like Jade does when working with companies like Nike, Sephora, and Adobe, as well as in her new book *Words to Live By*) and working with flowers. Moving each stem around to make sure the lines and negative space around each bloom are harmonious, balanced, and symmetrical in the blooms' own asymmetry is very similar to the letter spacing I used to aim for when I worked with typography as a graphic designer.

When I started thinking of tastemakers for this book, Jade was at the top of my list. I absolutely wanted to create something using the color palettes and the graphic style that had inspired me so much. I didn't know Jade, but when her agent immediately helped us book a date in mid-March of 2020, I was beyond thrilled and so honored. I believe the entire world knows what then happened in New York in March of 2020; needless to say, our shoot got postponed.

After being locked up for months, we were finally able to reschedule and wrap up the book late in the fall. After not being able to work on-site with flowers for so long, I kind of lost control and went nuts at the market gathering flowers for Jade's Brooklyn apartment. The result was an all-out, super bold, mini floral installation to interplay with a few of Jade's paintings. Sourcing the flowers and creating this piece was like getting drunk on color and flowers. After all those dark and dreary months, creating this color explosion felt fantastic.

I decided to make five individual pieces that could be pushed together to create one cohesive moment, but could also be pulled out individually. To offset and connect the colorful and bold arrangements, I added some lighter blush tones in various spots. For all of the arrangements, I used white ceramic vases in various geometric shapes as a way to connect the pieces.

A Bold
Floral Moment
Using Various
Techniques

Bright Red Ikebana-Inspired Arrangement in a Low Ceramic Vase

WHAT I USED:

1 low ceramic bowl with an approximate 7"-wide opening prepared with a flower frog as shown on page 126; 1 anthurium; 3 red nerines; 2 stems crocosmia; 4 dahlias; 4 roses; 4–6 peach ranunculus; 1–3 red ranunculus (preferably bicolored)

HOW I MADE IT:

This is yet another ikebana-inspired arrangement. On page 125 I show you how to put it together.

Small Blue Arrangement in a White Ceramic Vase

WHAT I USED:

1 small ceramic vase with an approximate 2–3"-wide opening prepared with chicken wire as shown on page 133; 2–3 hyacinths; 2–3 blue gentians; 1–3 larkspur

HOW I MADE IT:

For this casual little arrangement, I started with the gentians to set the height. Then I added the hyacinths, the shorter one up front. The larkspur went in last.

Bright Yellow Ikebana-Inspired Arrangement in a Footed Ceramic Bowl

WHAT I USED:

1 footed ceramic vase with an approximate 7–8"-wide opening prepared with a flower frog as shown on page 126; 6–8 yellow pom pom dahlias; 4–5 ranunculus in various yellow shades; 1 stem amaryllis; 1 peach garden rose; Chinaberry

HOW I MADE IT:

This is a fuller version of my ikebana-inspired arrangements. On page 125 I show you how to put it together.

Magenta-Colored Full Arrangement in a Round Ceramic Bowl

WHAT I USED:

1 low ceramic tray with an approximate 5–7"-wide opening fitted with Floral Base as shown on page 151; 4 magenta dahlias; 1 peach dahlia; 3 anemones; 3 stems stock; 5 pom pom dahlias; 4 tulips; 7 ranunculus in various pink tones; 5 spider mums; 5 hanging amaranthus; 3–4 bicolored carnations

HOW I MADE IT:

This was the first time I worked with Floral Base, a new product I was happy to test. The block allows you to add flowers all around to create a really lush look. On page 150 I write more about working with this product.

Anthony D'Argenzio

CONTENT CREATOR

Changing with the seasons, flowers offer a sense of time and place, especially in the home: a garden rose on a hot summer day, a dahlia in the fall, or a pop of purple crocuses on a cold winter day. Wherever present, flowers transport the mind, uplift the spirit, and add a sense of beauty.

It's in the little moments that flowers can give us the most. When given to a companion as a sign of love, placed at a bedside to make a guest feel welcome, or brought as a gesture of appreciation to someone you know or have never met. They bloom as fast as they wilt, so let's take a moment to appreciate flowers and their versatile beauty. —ANTHONY

A few years ago, I was invited to participate in Design*Sponge, the iconic but recently closed blog created by Grace Bonney. Back then, they ran a series of portraits where artists and designers shared what went on in an ordinary day. It was called *A Day in the Life Of*. As it turned out, Anthony's story and mine ran back-to-back.

Anthony had such impeccable taste and style and I really admired the way he had renovated and restored his Manhattan apartment. Like most city apartments, it was small, but so warm and effortlessly furnished—super authentic. Soon thereafter, I discovered his Instagram feed. There is something about Anthony's photos that captivates your eye and draws you in. There is a mystery to them, a story you want to explore.

When I approached Anthony about my book idea, I knew he was also into flowers—he followed me on Instagram—and what person with good taste, a sense of style, and an appreciation of beauty wouldn't be?

Anthony has since moved to Hudson, a small former mill and whaling town in Upstate New York that has managed to undergo a gradual transformation without losing any of its charm and authenticity. With one of the longest main streets in the Hudson Valley, it bustles with energy and hosts an astonishing number of artists and creative types. It's a perfect spot for Anthony's newest venture: This Old Hudson, a growing collection of historic properties that he renovates, curates, and rents as studio space, or for gatherings of all sorts. At the time of our visit, his company, Zio and Sons, had just released a beautiful collection of porcelain tiles that were showcased in kitchens and baths.

Through his work as a content creator, Anthony knows how to tell a story through images and vignettes. Strolling through the homes he has restored, you find yourself wondering who else has walked these narrow hallways, climbed these stairs, shared meals here, and slept in these rooms.

I wanted my flowers to add to these stories and create a sense of wonder, be rich and lush. As a contrast, I also wanted to create an arrangement of bud vases, to show Anthony's cool, minimalistic side.

The fact that Cedar Farms, a great local wholesaler and farm, is practically next door made sourcing so much easier. Interestingly, one of my freelancers works there. She drove me around the farm and I would pick whatever I wanted, including gorgeous tomatillos and dried weeds. Soon Anthony's bathroom sink was filled with thirsty flowers waiting to be arranged.

"It's in the little moments that flowers can give us the most." —ANTHONY

Garden Roses and Wildflowers in a Rustic Cast-Iron Vase (next page)

To capture the space and the essence of Hudson, and to stand out in this historic and rich environment, I wanted to create an arrangement with a lot of depth and texture. I also wanted to stick to Anthony's favorite colors, yellow and light green, and include garden roses, grasses, and wildflowers—blooms he had told me he liked.

Since Anthony lives and works a couple of hours away from my studio, I made this arrangement on-site, using a really heavy cast-iron urn I brought from home. These rustic arrangements are so timeless and satisfying to make and beautiful to look at. They fit in almost everywhere in your home, and once you get the hang of it, the combinations of blooms are virtually limitless.

Here we have used a pretty large number of different blooms, but you can use whatever is at hand and scale it to your own conditions. And don't forget Mother Nature! Foraging where it is allowed is the best way to start.

WHAT I USED:

1 heavy cast-iron vase with an approximate 10–12"-wide opening prepared with chicken wire as shown on page 133; 3 cream garden roses; 3 peach garden roses; 8–10 yellow and purple ranunculus; 5–6 blush snapdragons; 3 cream and purple phlox; 6 white sweet peas; 4 cream scabiosas; 6 cream or white lisianthus; 6 yellow and burgundy zinnias; 5 breadseed rattle poppy; 1 green persimmon; Mixed wild foliage such as sea oats, bupleurum, "Love in a Puff" balloon vines, and catmint. On page 133, you can read more about how I approach large and loose arrangements like this.

Effortless Tablescape with Local Farm Flowers

Tablescapes are all about texture and scale, and there are no real rules! You can make a really pretty arrangement using just three small vases, or you can cover a long table or a mantelpiece with a variety of bottles and vases. Adding small art objects, or items with special meaning, help tell the story.

Here I mixed plain glass bottles with some of Anthony's own pieces, like the Picasso vase, designed by Frances Palmer, a Connecticut-based ceramic artist. This vase is so pretty I wish I owned it!

To keep it minimal, we stuck to glass and white ceramic vases, and the same color palette we used in the large arrangement.

WHAT I USED:

1 large, white ceramic pitcher with an approximate 6"-wide opening; 1 medium-size white ceramic vase with an approximate 4–5"-wide opening; 3 small glass bottles

Arrangements, left to right:

2 "Love in a Puff" balloon vines in a medium-size ceramic vase; 3 zinnias in a glass bottle; 2 sweet peas in a glass bottle; Foraged weeds from the farm in a small white ceramic vase; See page 146 for more about how I approach bud vase arrangements.

Kate Shelter

ARTIST

Flowers are my ritual—bringing the outdoors inside—and the subject of my watercolor paintings and oversize geranium and poppy murals. My studio is two blocks from the New York City flower market. I take pleasure in going weekly to Dutch Flower Line on 28th Street, where I often bump into Ingrid, to select one type of cut flowers, whichever catches my eye: coral peonies, white anemones, pink ranunculus, or an armful of smiling chamomile . . . heaven is a room full of flowers.

I carry them home, like a baby swaddled in my arms, and get them into water; divide, clip, and dunk them into my collection of vases and vessels, and place them on our Scandinavian pine dining table. Inspired by the flowers' colors, I set the table for the week with a similar palette of linens, napkins, candles, and plates.

I then grab as many arrangements I can carry—slim stem vases and large flower bombs of blush dahlias—and bring them into my studio, where I paint them from multiple angles, as much as time will allow. It's a race against the blossom. Flowers light a fire under me. I feel compelled to paint as much as possible while the blooms peak. After they die, I start all over again with a trip to 28th Street. —KATE

"My ritual of designing the table with flowers starts the week fresh and connects me with nature." —KATE

I first met Kate at an art gallery where she was showing her watercolors and I had made the flower arrangements for the opening night. I admired her work and she liked my flowers, so we started talking.

Painting flowers is one of Kate's many skills, and her illustrations have been shown in *Vogue*, *Vanity Fair*, the *New York Times*, and *Elle*—everywhere you would want your work to be seen. She also runs her own luxury brand consultancy, writes books, and collaborates with cool designers like Veronica Beard, and Good Samaritans like Toms.

And she paints, a lot, both artistically and commercially. I love the way Kate captures flowers, vibrant and alive, with no two blooms looking exactly alike—perfect in their own imperfection. Some of her paintings remind me of the old-school botanical prints I have in my studio. Her art is organic and vivid, but the colors are often limited to a very few.

It is not unlike the way I see flowers, where the beauty is often found in the imperfect and unpredictable way they bud, blossom, and wilt. The bud that never opened, the wilted leaf that is all curled up, or the twisted stem that refuses to follow the others—they are all part of a natural process that cannot be stopped but, for those with an artistic eye, it can be captured through art and photography.

Kate's Chelsea loft maintains a perfect balance between the traditional and the modern—a lived-in, classic look that will never be outdated. The open-concept layout and large cast-iron windows give the space a cool and contemporary look, but it is appointed with a lot of antiques, some from Kate's family, and the furniture is upholstered in her favorite colors: pink and green.

It is beautiful and feminine without being fussy, a fun and welcoming home for a family of three—soon to be four!

As evident in her watercolors, Kate loves peonies, and who doesn't? They are among the prettiest and most useful blooms, since they can make even the smallest arrangement look full and lush. But she also told me she likes roses, ranunculus, chamomile, Queen Anne's lace, and geraniums.

Bringing flowers to this space would be easy!

Pink Peonies in a
Porcelain Bowl

For the dining room, I decided to play off
the colors in the painting and make a lush
ikebana-inspired arrangement using pink
peonies, similar to the ones in Kate's painting,
tulips, larkspur buds, and geranium leaves.
The vase is an inexpensive florist's footed
bowl. The blue edge and pattern evoke her
watercolors, and it works really well here.
These arrangements are so pretty and super
easy to make at home, using less material,
but still achieving a big impact.

WHAT I USED:

1 extra large bowl with an approximate
9–10"-wide opening prepared with a
flower frog, see page 126; 4 Coral Charm
peonies; 5 pink double tulips (hiding in the
back); 3 stems pink didiscus; 5 larkspur
buds; 1 pink cornflower; Begonia leaves.
See page 125 for more about how I
approach ikebana-inspired arrangements.

Summer Blooms in a Footed Vase

For the living room, I wanted to create a loose assembly of summer blooms, like an overgrown meadow captured in a frame. To complement Kate's décor, I chose a vintage footed silver vase I had in the studio. I often work with footed vases and bowls. It makes it easier to achieve the right balance between height and width, and it allows longer stems to arch without hitting the surface beneath.

WHAT I USED:

1 footed vase with an approximate 7–8"-wide opening prepared with chicken wire as shown on page 133; 2 large yellow peonies; 5 white ranunculus; 5 dark red lisianthus; 3 light pink lilacs; 2 light yellow tulips; 3 buttercup stems; 5 red cornflowers; 5 white sweet peas. See page 133 for more about how I approach large and loose arrangements like this.

> "Using flowers is a way we can honor what has been given to us by Mother Earth."
> —FREDRIK

Fredrik Berselius

CHEF & OWNER AT ASKA

Flowers add a fresh perspective to the stories I want to tell; they help me remember my childhood and places I have traveled. They bring back memories from Sweden, like picking flowers for my teacher at the end of the school year, a ritual I cherished and that I want my guests to experience.

Like all ingredients, flowers follow the seasons, starting with tree flowers in the spring. Summer flowers are full of flavor and beauty, which can be captured and preserved by using traditional methods, like pickling and drying. We add the dried and pickled flowers to our recipes, but also use them to infuse oils and vinegars. —FREDRICK

To be successful, tablescape décor should complement the food and not distract from it, so using a mix of foraged greens, dried grasses, and white single blooms felt like the right choice for this minimally decorated room.

To play off Fredrik's menu, which is made up of a dozen small dishes, I decided to place twelve small arrangements on the table. Using fishing wire, we also hung some branches from the ceiling to create the illusion of walking through a Swedish forest.

"Mr. Berselius is the rare chef who thinks like an artist and gets away with it," wrote the food critic Pete Wells in the *New York Times*. Fredrik's restaurant, Aska, had just opened at its new location in a restored warehouse building in Williamsburg, Brooklyn, and everyone was eager to find out if he had managed to elevate his distinctive take on Nordic cuisine to a new and even higher level.

He had.

"Having dinner" at Aska is an experience like no other, an adventure rather than a meal. As one dish after another is set in front of you as part of a twelve-course tasting menu, you feel like you have been taken on a journey through the woods and waters of Sweden and the northeastern United States.

And flowers are everywhere! Here, they don't just act as décor; they are an essential part of the way Fredrik thinks, prepares, cooks, and plates.

At first sight, his dishes may look simple in their minimalism, but there is nothing simple or simplistic about the way Fredrik approaches culinary arts. On the contrary, the process, for which he has been awarded two Michelin stars, is complex and represents the cutting edge of art and science.

Since we would be working in a dining room, it seemed natural to create a tablescape and use mostly what grows in the parks and forests where Fredrik is known to forage, like Queen Anne's lace, pine, ferns, and grasses.

I also kept the fresh flowers to a single color: white. It is dark inside Aska's dining room. The walls are black like the ceilings and most of the furniture. The only things that gleam are the small copper pots they use.

Since this was once a commercial warehouse, the ceilings are super high, so to create a more intimate mood, I decided to add a natural-looking overhead installation that we would suspend from the ceiling using Command hooks and fishing line. This would create a feeling of having dinner in the woods.

Forest Inspired Tablescape Detail

WHAT I USED:

1 paperwhite in a glass bottle; **4** white *Lysimachia* in a brown ceramic vase with an approximate 1"-wide opening; **1** juniper berry branch in a cream-colored ceramic vase with an approximate ½"-wide opening; **4** flannel flowers and **1** *Heuchera* leaf in a round ceramic bowl with an approximate 3"-wide opening; **1** dried agapanthus

When it comes to bud or small vase arrangements, mixing different materials adds an element of surprise, like here where I have mixed ceramics and glass with wood. The wood vase, hand-turned from one piece of wood by Oakland-based artist Melanie Abrantes, has a small glass vial inside that protects it.

Foraged Evergreens and Tall Grasses in a Ceramic Vase

To add to the feeling of having dinner in the woods, I made a large arrangement using pine branches as a base, and added some tall grasses.

WHAT I USED:

1 ceramic vase with an approximate 6"-wide opening prepared with twigs as shown on page 138; 3 *Lindera* branches; 3 black *Ligustrum* berries; 2 green *Pittosporum*s; 10–12 ruby silk love grass; 8 fountain grass; 5 pine branches

HOW I MADE IT:

Using twigs instead of chicken wire to keep the stems in place is a technique I started using a while ago and really like. In this case, I filled the lower half of the vase with twigs. See page 137 for more about how I do it.

Dried, Fresh, and Foraged Flowers in a Low Ceramic Bowl

I love it when the vase has a story to tell. With this one, the story goes back to the ancient French village of Saint-Amand-en-Puisaye, where potters have been at work since the middle ages. Nicole Hurtault and her brother Claude, owners of Les Guimards, now carry on this tradition. While still hand throwing every piece and quarrying the same clay that has been used for generations, they also experiment with new glazes and colors for a modern look.

WHAT I USED:
> 1 vase with an approximate 5–6"-wide opening prepared with a flower frog as shown on page 126; 2 fresh paperwhites; 3 fresh white *Lysimachias*; 2 dried agapanthus; 1 dried oak branch; 2 dried strawflowers; 2–3 dried umbrella ferns; 1–2 dried *Grevillea* "Ivanhoe"; 1 dried natural tallow berry; 1–2 dried lacecap hydrangeas; 2 fresh *Alliums*; Fountain grass

"Flowers for me evoke memories and their presence in a room has always demanded attention." —VIRGINIA

Virginia Sin

CERAMICIST

I find that most of my inspirations come from memories. I would say a lot of my work is deeply personal and nostalgic. Flowers—just the act of looking at their beauty—bring me such joy. They remind me that everything has a life cycle and that it's important to embrace all we have, because that too is fleeting, so we'd better take a good glimpse.
—VIRGINIA

When I stepped into her Brooklyn apartment, hauling four buckets of flowers and everything else we would need for the photo shoot, Virginia and I had actually never met! We had been bouncing ideas back and forth for a few weeks and had come up with a story we both wanted to tell and a style and concept that felt right in her minimalist space and would enhance the ceramic vases she designs. So, on a certain level we knew each other. The fact that we had both built successful careers and business from our side hustles made for another point of connection.

Contemporary and locally made ceramics have seen quite a revival, and I find myself more and more drawn to these vases and bowls. The color of kiln-dried natural clay is not only attractive, it works well in so many settings and with a variety of color palettes. Virginia's playful and beautifully crafted vases are such great examples of this trend. They are totally unique and speak exclusively for her, which is of course why her business is so tremendously successful.

The apartment, which Virginia shares with her husband, is located in a historic landmark building located right on the waterfront in the Williamsburg section of Brooklyn. The Egyptian revival–style building, which once housed the biggest grocery chain in the country as well as a bourbon distillery, has floor-to-ceiling factory windows and is flooded with light. The apartment is sparsely but beautifully furnished in earthy colors with blue accents.

Virginia had told me artists such as Richard Serra, who liked to explore the relationships between art and space, and the simple esthetic of the Bauhaus movement, inspired her. She also said she liked periwinkle blue next to terra-cotta and had always been drawn to wabi-sabi, the Japanese design philosophy that focuses on finding beauty within the imperfections of life and the natural cycle of growth and decay, something I always try to achieve in my arrangements.

I had a pretty good idea of how to incorporate these ideas in a few arrangements that would allow me to play with weight, balance, and gravity, a sense I get from her vases. For my color palette, I would stick to blues, yellows, and orange—the colors of the apartment décor—and not add a lot of greens. Since Virginia grew up in Southern California, where her mother grew bird-of-paradise flowers in their front yard, bringing some of them was a given. They would add personal meaning to my arrangement and look great in one of the vases I had decided to use, the sculptural two-piece Doline.

At first, working with a minimalist concept can seem limiting for a florist, but it actually isn't. It frees you from a lot of choices and preconceived ideas about arranging flowers, such as that an arrangement has to be "lush" and include a ton of different blooms to have an impact, and lets you create something equally impactful using less, focusing instead on the form and essence of the flower itself.

I love this vase! Virginia named it Doline, and since I am the daughter of a geologist, I happen to know that it is another term for a sinkhole, a perfect name for this fun and versatile piece, which, like my flowers, plays with gravity and balance.

Ikebana-Inspired Arrangement in Virginia's Pillow Talk Vase

I love everything about this little vase. Designed in the shape of a pillow, with rows of small openings, it functions both as a vessel and a flower frog and is a florist's dream.

No prep work, just pour the water and you have a perfect base for a sweet ikebana-style arrangement. To complement the apartment décor, I chose grape hyacinths and *Nigella* damascena, a flower I love for the tiny leaves, called bracts, that surround the flower, the soft blue color, and the little seedpods. I pushed most of the stems into one single hole, believe it or not!

You can create this same arrangement in a low bowl with an approximate 4–6"–wide opening, like the Ikebana-Inspired Arrangement Using Flower Frog as shown on page 125, leaving lots of empty space around the flowers.

WHAT I USED:

1 grape hyacinth; 3 *Nigellas*; 1 poppy pod; 1 *Lindera* branch

Poppies in Virginia's Cenote Vase

Some flowers work especially well in single ingredient arrangements where each one of them can play a solo part, like poppies, with their crepe-paper-like petals and wiry stems. The cool cylinder-shaped vase I chose had an organic texture and handmade feel to it, and the holes on the sides allowed me to insert flowers at a lower level, creating an illusion of the stems actually growing out of the vase—an idea I loved.

WHAT I USED:

1 cylinder-shaped ceramic vase with an approximate 3.5"-wide opening; 15 poppies in various shades of orange and pink

HOW I MADE IT:

This vase was really tall—taller than my poppies—so to be able to use it I invented a whole new technique: the "soda bottle with a flower frog attached." First, I cut the neck off a water bottle, and cut a hole in the top and threaded a wire through (to make it easy to remove from the vase by simply pulling on the wire). I then attached a frog to the bottom of the bottle, and finally I added rocks to the bottom of the water bottle, to weigh it down and give a bit more height.

For this kind of arrangement, I like to start with the tallest stems to determine the height and shape of my arrangement. Then, as I turn the vase, I place the other stems, one by one, where they will get a chance to show off the most.

Michael Diaz-Griffith

ANTIQUES EXPERT

Flowers are one of the most important elements at any event, and at an affair like The Winter Show, they take on a heightened importance. When the flowers are revealed at The Winter Show's Opening Night Party each year, there is an audible buzz. It is a direct response to beauty, but it's also the sound of comprehension: "Ah, this is what the Show is about this year." It's a vision statement in petals, stems, foliage, and fruit.

The flowers express the fair's ever-evolving identity and perspective on beauty, rather than specific themes, and people follow their rather fluid evolution with great interest. Because they catalyze so much curiosity, flowers are the perfect vessel for brand storytelling. When the Show wanted to demonstrate its commitment to antiques and historic art, but also convey that it was committed to viewing history through a contemporary lens, Ingrid reconceptualized old masters' still lifes in our floral design. The resulting arrangements crystallized—in the most vivid, immediate, and visual of ways—the Show's direction: Minimalism was out; romance, whimsy, wit, and complexity were in.

Years later, people still ask me about those flowers. —MICHAEL

Making dreams come true is what I live for, and when I invited Michael to be one of my tastemakers, that is exactly what followed: With the help of some really good friends, his dream home became reality overnight.

Alas, the splendor was temporary, but for a magnificent moment, it was all there to love and behold: the rococo girandoles over the baby blue Egyptian-revival sofa, the art deco buffet table graced with a two-hundred-year-old giltwood neoclassical mirror, priceless art and artifacts to rest your eyes on, and vases that did not evoke a particular epoch, but actually originated in that time period.

To bring my flowers into this space was amazing, and arranging them in a bronze vase from 1830, almost unreal.

Michael and I are good friends. We met at The Winter Show, a yearly art event at the Park Avenue Armory, where the finest of the world's antiques experts get together to show off their treasures. Michael was the associate executive director there, and I was invited to design flower installations that would be there for the opening gala and stay fresh for the ten consecutive days the show went on.

Michael also cochaired The Young Collectors Night, a popular event where the current generation of collectors and art enthusiasts gathers to learn and discuss the wonders and pleasures of collecting whatever it is that captures their interest. In his new position, working for the London-based Sir John Soane's Museum, he will bring new experiences to this young and enthusiastic group.

Michael is an antiques expert with a capital *E*. His knowledge in this field is so broad and so deep that it just blows me away. To listen to him speak is to be transported to another world, where beauty rules, thoughts thrive, and quality wins over quantity every time. I knew from the start that I wanted to have Michael in my book, but I didn't know where we could photograph him. Like so many young New Yorkers, Michael and his husband resided in a small apartment—filled to the brim with their own personal treasures.

That's when the idea of designing Michael's dream space elsewhere arose. Since Michael knows absolutely everybody in this field, a location quickly materialized: The Gallery at 200 Lex, a sprawling indoor antiques gallery open to the public, with over fifty vendors, and literarily thousands of objects to choose from. Needless to say, Michael went to town.

The way Michael chooses an object to collect is a bit like I pick flowers to arrange: Take the most exquisite items you can find, put them together, and watch them interact. This approach, Michael has found, works as well in his closet as it does in his home. If you truly love everything you own, he says, everything will go together. I have found the same is often true with flowers.

In this spectacular setting, and with vases of such historical importance, I knew I wanted to go back in history for my inspiration as well. I would borrow my color palette from the Dutch masters, who ruled the world of art for much of the seventeenth century and whose still lifes still inspire, but in terms of composition, take cues from the more restrained neoclassical area, like a couple of eighteenth-century watercolor paintings by the French artist Jean-Jacques Avril.

"I love when a riot of color, or a romantic, maximalist detail, is set against a minimal backdrop—even in a painting from the seventeenth century, the juxtaposition feels fresh." —MICHAEL

Arrangement in an Antique Footed Bronze Vase

There are a million different reasons to admire the still lifes created by the Dutch masters: the play between light and shadow, the composition, the flowers, the odd accessories, the incredible richness of it all. But at the same time, it can feel a bit indulgent, decadent almost, to be working that way today. Wherever possible, I try to adhere to the idea that if you can achieve the same beauty and impact using less, you should. This approach also allows each bloom to show and not overwhelm the stunning vase and setting.

The vase I got to work with was one of a pair of 1830 bronze and sienna marble urns. It truly made a beautiful base for my flowers and contrasted with the playful white wooden geometrical and the empire mantel clock Michael had picked.

WHAT I USED:
1 antique vase with an approximate 8"-wide opening prepared with a flower frog as shown of page 126; 1 orange *Fritillaria imperialis*; 3 pink tulips; 1 red garden rose; 6 blush pink ranunculus; 3 white spray rose stems; 1 large begonia stem; 5 larkspur; 3 grape hyacinths; 3 orange carnations; 3 Didiscus lace flower; 2 white tweedia

Ikebana-Inspired Arrangement in a
Small Footed Marble Vase

Both the nineteenth-century marble vase and the Biedermeier mirror are from Sweden, one of my home countries, which made it extra special for me.

WHAT I USED:

1 small, footed vase with an approximate 3–4"–wide opening prepared with a flower frog as shown on page 126; 4 brown orchid blooms; 3 green and yellow Pom Pom ranunculus; 2 narcissuses; 5 grape hyacinths; 3 *Nigella* (love-in-a-mist)

Modern Take on Dutch Masters in a Cubist Vase

This wheel thrown vase designed by Brooklyn-born R. A. Pesce presented another really exciting opportunity for me to create something really big and beautiful. Though the shape and form could have lent itself to a variety of designs, I wanted to stick with my loose interpretation of the Dutch masters.

WHAT I USED:

1 large ceramic vase with an approximate 8"-wide opening prepared with chicken wire as shown on page 133; 2 orange *Fritillaria imperialis*; 10 salmon pink carnations; 5 salmon pink garden roses; 7 *Nigellas* (love-in-a-mist); 3 white narcissuses; 7 larkspur; 1 white spray rose; 2 blush tulips; 1 berry branch; 2 tweedias

"The ephemeral blooms in my garden take me to task. Their fleeting existence may come and go without ever being seen. But they don't mind. They are not asking to be seen or reminding me to look at them." —CORRIN

Corrin Arasa

FOUNDER & CREATIVE DIRECTOR AT PATINA STUDIOS

My daily practice is to see them, to see all the flowers—the ones growing in the ground, but also the ones in my children, in my husband, in strangers, in the world, and in myself. Their humble show of strength, after even the harshest of seasons, becomes a beacon of life for me, and I feel the comfort of the predictable pulse of time and nature. —CORRIN

Like myself, Corrin is part of the newish passion economy in which entrepreneurs build successful businesses doing what they love. Not always with the goal of becoming the biggest or the loudest, but rather the best and the happiest.

Over the years, working on a variety of events, I have collaborated with so many different vendors, and from the get-go, Patina Studios, an event design studio specializing in the newest and the hottest trends in staging and entertaining, stood out. Not only for the vintage furniture and accessories they offer, which are always fun and on trend, but even more so for the way they conduct their business.

In a trade with a lot of sharp elbows, Corrin and her crew are always kind and helpful and so much fun to work with. It is always about collaboration and getting the best result. When I started out making floral designs for weddings, it was often hard to find the sturdy wood tables I wanted to see my flowers on. So I started building them myself, using planks reclaimed from scaffolding.

They were pretty nice, and my clients liked them. As it turned out, so did Corrin. When I decided that the furniture building and rental business was not for me, she bought them. Corrin, who has a solid background in event planning, started her company in a smaller space in another part of Brooklyn. But as her business grew, and with it their inventory, they moved to Brooklyn Navy Yard, now a sought-after area located on the East River right between Dumbo and Williamsburg

For 165 years, Brooklyn Navy Yard was known as America's premier shipbuilding facility and some of our most famous warships, like the USS *Monitor*, was actually built and launched here.

After the Navy left Brooklyn in the sixties, the Navy Yard just sat there, taking up space on the coveted Brooklyn waterfront. Then someone had the splendid idea to convert the abandoned buildings into a mission-driven industrial park, primarily for small businesses. For Corrin, this was perfect.

The building that houses Patina Studios is pretty raw and you enter through the loading dock. Inside the walls are bare and the pipes exposed, but as soon as you step off the service elevator and enter the showroom, you are surrounded with loads of really cool furniture and interesting accents.

The whole place has a happy and creative vibe, and for our shoot, Corrin chose an updated glam-luxe seventies look. Using a space like this would allow me to show my new and edgy designs and use some really fun vases, like the hand-turned wooden vases from Melanie Abrantes and Matagalan Plantae's shapely clay vases.

Quaint Tablescape

Another area of the studio had been set up as a dining room, anchored by a set of art deco chairs that had been reupholstered in bright blue velvet. The beautifully preserved Paul Evans table was perfect for a small-scale tablescape. For this, I had decided to go for a similar selection of flowers to what I had used in the large arrangement and use a variety of small terracotta and wood vases. For fun I had also added some cherries and black raspberries that I threaded a wire through to create miniature sculptures.

WHAT I USED:

3 red clay or terra-cotta vases with approximately 2.5", 3", and 8"-wide openings in various heights; 1 brass bowl with an approximate 4"-wide opening; 1 tiny clay bowl with an approximate 2.5"-wide opening; 1 tiny vintage vase; 2 wooden vases with glass inserts

Arrangements, left to right:

1 black scabiosa, 1 brown cymbidium orchid in a low terra-cotta vase

1 ornamental hops; 5 peperomia "Emerald Ripple Red" leaves (from potted plant); 2 closed lotus flowers; 1 red ranunculus; 2 black scabiosa; 1 phalenopsis (from a potted plant)

Cherries and blackberries in and on top of various vases

See page 147 for more about how I approach bud and small vase arrangements.

Luxe, Lavish Arrangement in a Brass Bowl

For a living room vignette, Corrin had a wall painted teal, which provided a perfect backdrop to this rich and glam deluxe arrangement, using a large number of flowers in rich jewel tones.

WHAT I USED:

1 brass bowl with an approximate 10"-wide opening prepared with chicken wire as shown on page 133; 8–10 stems dark purple sweet peas; 1 brown orchid stem divided into shorter pieces; 12 dark burgundy or black ranunculus; 2 red spray rose stems; 3–4 dark purple tulips, flexed as shown on page 115; 3 purple mini *Anthuriums*; 6–7 Erica heather stems; Begonia leaves; Ligustrum berries; Dried eucalyptus. See page 133 for more about how I approach large and loose arrangements like this.

FLOWERS
AT HOME

When most of my business was put on pause due to the pandemic, I was forced to come up with new business ideas, just like so many others. Bloom Box, where my customers get to make their own arrangements using our carefully selected bunches of flowers and follow my instructions via a pre-recorded video, as well as live virtual classes, became a true blessing in disguise. It was inspiring to see how people took my ideas and made them their own, truly creating new and unique arrangements that fit their home and style. And I was so thrilled to be able to offer flowers that many might not be able to get their hands on otherwise. Here are a few examples of at-home arrangements.

Brittney

"I am at home with my two little kids right now and having fresh flowers around the house is the best way to brighten my days. I have an organic approach when it comes to my home and flowers; I often mix a few stems from my local flower shop with anything that grows in my garden. I loved this color palette and decided to make a romantic arrangement to put in my baby girl's room. The white Frances Palmer Trapezoid vase, a favorite of mine, with its lovely handmade qualities, is perfect for this style. To me, it makes total sense to place flowers in the nursery, since I am there all the time and it is nice to look at while I feed and rock her to sleep."

Brittney's Arrangement

1 white vase, 4" wide; 3 delphiniums; 2 privet berry; 3 tweedia; 3 pieris; 1 white anemone; 3 rice flowers; 5 forget-me-nots; 4 lisanthus; 5 white sweet peas; 5 white ranunculus; 5 tulips. For instructions on how to make an arrangement using chicken wire, see page 133.

Eva

"As a collaborator on Ingrid's books, I have learned a lot from watching her work her magic. But until now, I have actually never attempted to make anything more advanced than cutting supermarket flowers to different heights and sticking them in a vase, or foraging in my backyard. I am sloppy by nature and my patience typically runs low. But following a step-by-step video, using the flower frog and chicken wire method, and really focusing on doing every step as shown, it was actually much easier than I thought. And fun! The low, footed brass bowl is a reused florist vase that Ingrid lent me. I worked on it on my kitchen island, which was a perfect height for me. The only thing missing was a lazy Susan to spin the flowers around as I arranged them. That would have been really helpful."

Eva's Arrangement

1 brass vase, 6–7" wide; 2 cappuccino roses; 3 peach ilex berry stems; 5 white ranunculus; 5 white tweedia; 1 golden mustard rose; 3 cream spray roses; 3 mauve astrantia; 5 mauve lisianthus; 5 princess tulips, flexed; 6 autumn eucalyptus; Garden greens. For instructions on how to make an arrangement using chicken wire and a flower frog, see page 144.

Molly

"As a designer, I often work on photo shoots and I have learned a lot from watching florists at work. Even though I love bringing anything that grows in the garden into my house, I often feel a bit intimidated when it comes to arranging flowers in a traditional way. I am more into free-flowing design, and I like the idea of mixing flowers of different heights, similar to bud vase arrangements. I have a slew of different vases and bowls around the house, and while we were playing around for the photos, I ended up putting a clear glass sphere bud vase inside a super-tall fluted vase so the flowers would appear to be floating in midair. This felt like a great way to create volume with just a few stems. It was so fun that both my daughters joined in as well! They made sweet little ikebana-inspired arrangements using flower frogs. In the process, they spontaneously decided to make cute little floral headpieces for themselves as well."

Isa's Ikebana-Style Arrangement

1 low bowl or vase, 4-5" wide; 6 lavender clematis; 2 lavender ranunculus; 6 purple anemone; 4 pink dahlias; 1 cream carnation

For instructions on how to make ikebana-style arrangements, see pages 125–129.

TECHNIQUES
&
RECIPES

HOW I THINK AND PUT IT ALL TOGETHER

A famous chef once said that the hardest part about writing recipes for his staff is the variation in the ingredients themselves. You don't always know exactly how big a carrot is, he explained, the level of sweetness of your strawberries, or how much water the potatoes will retain. I personally find that strict recipes and detailed instructions are inhibiting, and that what goes for cooking pretty much goes for flowers, so I prefer to use recipes as loose guidelines and inspiration.

No two peonies are exactly alike, and there is no way of knowing if the tulips will be the same shade as they were the last time we bought them. This is the "charm" of working with living things, and it never gets old. At the studio, we never use recipes, not even for our big events, when we create hundreds of arrangements. Even if we could, we wouldn't want all of the arrangements to look exactly alike, just related.

Floral design is an art form. I don't think a florist should be stifled by having to follow a strict recipe—and neither should you. So instead of telling you exactly how long to cut each stem or how many filler flowers to add, I will try to share how I think and work instead—how I put it all together.

Arranging flowers should be fun, like painting a picture, and you should allow yourself to mess up and start over. As I like to say to my students: Never be afraid! The way we work, there is a lot of room for "error." Keep moving your flowers around until you are happy.

In this chapter, I will explain how I look for proportion and balance rather than perfection, and how I change and adjust what I am doing as I work. For clarity, I will write how many of each flower, twig, or stem I used for the arrangement pictured, and the approximate size of the vase. But I want you to see this as a guide rather than a recipe, and you will surely want to add or subtract and move things around to achieve the look you want.

Flowers are wild and unpredictable and for me, working with them is a creative process rather than a set of steps. Your arrangement may look very different from the one I made for the photo, but it will be beautiful, and it will be yours.

THE ART OF PICKING FLOWERS

Before there can be any arranging, there must be flowers, and how you choose and care for them is the most important aspect of the whole process. As a floral designer, I have the luxury of picking and choosing the best from a huge indoor market where almost anything is available and everything is fresh. I love going there in the morning, before the big rush, when all the buckets are full.

Whenever possible, I try to use locally grown flowers, and what is naturally in season. At the market, I always look for the growers and farms I know. Their flowers are always the most tempting and every once in a while, I treat myself to a bunch just because I can't resist them. The most addictive ones are the bicolored or peach ranunculus from Hautau & Sons in New Jersey. The owners, Brian and Kimberly, have the most amazing eye for color and their blooms basically do all the work for me. Buying local is not only best for the planet we all share, but it also means that my flowers have not been sitting in a box for days. Flowers look so much prettier when they maintain their natural shape..

For many of you, the selection may be more limited, and when nothing is growing outside, you may only have access to a local flower shop, supermarket, or corner deli. Even if your flowers come to you prepackaged in cellophane wrap, always examine them first.

Are they flat on one side? Not good.

Do you see any loose, discolored, or wilted petals or leaves? I usually turn the bunch upside down and give them a gentle shake. If petals fall out, the flowers are usually not fresh. Another great trick is to take a quick whiff and see if the bunch smells moldy or off.

And while you have them upside down, check to see if the stems look suspicious. They should be green or white. If they are brownish, yellowing, or soft, they are about to go bad. But even if they have the right color, make sure they don't look like they have been squeezed or pressed too tightly together during transport.

Bleached flowers are surprisingly trendy right now, I see them everywhere, and while I don't want to point fingers, I do everything I can to avoid them. While they may seem tempting, I think you should know that they have been soaked in a bleach bath three to four times. This is not a sustainable choice.

YOUR MAIN CHARACTERS

What types of flowers you want and how many of each to get depends on what kind of arrangement you are planning to make. When I select flowers for larger arrangements, I look at them as characters in a play where everyone has a different role. Some are bigger, others smaller, but they all deserve a chance to show off and shine.

Foliage: Foliage is essential when creating wild and loose arrangements. The amount and types used will depend on the vibe you are going for. I usually like to use more than one variety in the same arrangement. I also love to forage whenever it can be done responsibly. This gives my arrangements a personal touch, and brings back memories from my days in Sweden living closer to nature. Grasses, rosebush vines, and ferns are versatile and wildly available. I also love branches and twigs of all kinds. Vines are harder to get year-round. They drape so beautifully, and I love when I find them. Eucalyptus, which comes in countless varieties, is accessible and always a favorite, both for its scent and the way the stems arch. Many potted plants, like geraniums, hellebores, and various heucheras often make it into my arrangements as well.

Face focal flower: The star of the show and the one in the limelight. This should be a large-headed bloom, like a peony, dahlia, or garden rose. If you can't find a bloom that contrasts in size to the other flowers, I suggest creating a group of three or so flowers to create a graphic moment.

Base flower: Pretty character actors that add depth to the arrangement. Spray roses are really versatile, as are carnations, hellebore, cosmos, and lisianthus.

Gestural flower: Supporting roles that add height and interest and prevent the arrangement from looking too perfect and symmetrical. I love anything with a stem that has a pretty curvature, such as my favorite: local ranunculus.

Textural flower: Some florists call these "fillers," but don't think of these as extras! They are just as important as the rest of the crew. I usually add them last to finish off my arrangement and make sure there are no holes in it. Astrantia, tweedia, and nigella are perfect for this, as are thistles, seedheads, and all kinds of fruit and berry twigs.

Sometimes I follow these rules and have all my characters in place, but just as often, I break all the rules and go with my gut. And at the end of the day, I want them all to win an Oscar!

CARING FOR FLOWERS

If there are two things flowers dislike, it is excessive heat and a lack of water, and in order to get the most out of our blooms, we keep them well hydrated and cool.

When the flowers get to the studio, they have often been boxed up for a day or two. As soon as they arrive, we unwrap them, cut the stems, remove all leaves that would be below water level, and put them in water. Then we let them drink for the rest of the day—often longer—before arranging them.

While hydrating, flowers do best in the right water temperature:

- Flowers with soft stems, such as tulips, daffodils, and irises, like cold water.
- Flowers with medium-soft stems, such as carnations, mums, lilies, and peonies, like lukewarm water.
- Flowers with hard or woody stems, such as roses, lilacs, and hydrangeas, like warm water. To maximize their ability to absorb water, you can dip the tips of the stems in about an inch of boiling water for thirty seconds before putting them in water. This will kill bacteria and also help revive them if they look wilted. Just make sure to point the blooms away from the steam.

When the flowers are fully hydrated and you are ready to arrange them, luke-warm water works for everything. I also like to add plant food to the water. It provides important nourishment and kills harmful bacteria that make flowers wilt prematurely.

In the studio, we keep the flowers in a small walk-in cooler. At home, you should store your flowers in the coolest area of the house or apartment overnight, or when you are not enjoying them. Outside is fine as long as the temperature does not dip below freezing. You should also be mindful of drafts.

Tip: Everybody loves peonies, from their tight little buds to their spectacular blooms. But sometimes it seems the flowers get stuck in the bud phase and fail to open. This is due to a sticky, sugary coating, which in nature is polished off by hungry ants. At home you can help your peonies along by spraying them or dunking the whole bud in lukewarm water then shaking off the excess water—this will help them open faster.

FLEXING TULIPS

Tip: Opening, or flexing, your tulips is a nice way to create more volume with a single bloom. To do this, hold the blossom in one hand while carefully bending the petals away from the bottom, one by one.

PICKING THE RIGHT VASE

When I started out and Tin Can Studios was brand new, I hardly ever bought vases. I preferred to use all kinds of cans, urns, bottles, and glasses that I found here and there and often refurbished and repurposed. It became a thing and, in the early days, a part of my brand.

I still like to repurpose vases and use the same ones over again, and when I meet with a new client, I always ask them if they have any vases from their collection we can use. This will not only add a personal touch to the overall look but will also adhere to our philosophy of not buying things we don't need and adding to the pile of stuff. As my business has grown and come to include a much wider range of clients and venues, I have branched out in this area as well. As a result, I have had the honor to create arrangements in everything from crystal vases from Lalique and porcelain from de Gournay to giant neoclassical urns from Sotheby's. This fits my philosophy of sustainability perfectly.

I can't overstate the importance of the vase you pick. Not just for the look of the vase itself, but for the scale and proportions of the arrangement. There is no right and wrong here, but the same arrangement can and will look completely different depending on the vase you ultimately choose.

For my wide and loose arrangements, I like the flowers to be twice as high and wide as the vase. In other words, two-thirds flowers to one-third vase. For these, I often choose a footed vase. There is something so graceful and pretty about those vases, and it allows stems to arch over the edge without touching the surface below.

When arranging flowering branches or long berry stems, a tall ceramic vase looks great. I still want more flowers than vase, though.

For an ikebana-inspired arrangement, I love low bowls to show off the sculptural qualities of each flower, and for bud vase arrangements, you want to mix it up with varying sizes and shapes.

Ceramics have become really popular and I love taking advantage of the many talented ceramic artists we have right here in Brooklyn. Like Virginia Sin, who is featured as a tastemaker in this book; Wilcoxson Brooklyn Ceramics, who designed a really pretty vase we now use for our single arrangement deliveries; Aviva Rowley, who used to work as a freelance florist for me and who makes some amazing sculptural vases; and Erin Banta Wilford at WrenLab Ceramics, to name a few. Local antiques dealers, like Barbara Israel in New York, are also great for supplying those one-of-a-kind cast-iron and brass urns my clients love.

Antique and vintage vases will always have a special place in my heart and whenever they fit into a concept, I incorporate them. They have soul and character and using the same ones over and over instead of buying new all the time is a beautiful way for me to reduce my carbon footprint.

When working with antiques or vessels not designed as vases, always make sure they can hold water. If not, you can line them with a smaller container that won't leak.

Another important consideration when picking the vase is the space the arrangement will be displayed in and the surface it will stand on. A glass shelf in a modern gallery calls for a different vase than a marble mantel in a mansion or a farm table in a rustic wedding venue, and sometimes the juxtaposition of an antique urn in a super-modern space can achieve just the right effect. This all depends on the concept and look you are going for. I usually like marrying pieces from different eras as it lets our minds travel in time and allows for more personal expression.

MY TECHNIQUES

Chicken wire is inexpensive and one of the most useful tools to have around. Arranging flowers using chicken wire is my most popular method. The chicken wire can also be reshaped and used over and over. The netlike openings are perfectly sized and shaped to keep most stems in place while still allowing you to move them around and work in a more painterly way.

> **WHEN I USE IT:** I find it particularly useful when I am creating looser and wilder arrangements with flowers and foliage arching over the edges of the container. If the stems are tiny, I just pinch the chicken wire into the right shape, and when I am dealing with really large stems, I use wire cutters to create a larger opening. Just be sure to bend the wire inward, so you don't rip the stem when inserting it.

Flower frogs, or kenzan, come in a wide range of sizes and styles and are both easy to use and versatile. They also allow you to move your flowers really easily.

> **WHEN I USE THEM:** When I make ikebana-inspired arrangements. They are great for keeping branches and twigs in place, and also come in handy when I need to add a bit of weight to a vase to prevent it from tipping over. When working with really tiny stems that don't stay in place between the pins, I cover them with stem wrap before inserting them.

Twigs, yes, ordinary twigs you find outside, can be used instead of chicken wire— just make sure they are thin and bendy so you can shape them as you wish.

> **WHEN I USE THEM:** To create loose and natural-looking arrangements.

Lazy Susans are incredibly useful, I have loads of these small turntables in the studio and I use them for every arrangement I make, and with almost every step of the process. If you plan to place your arrangement where it will be visible from every angle, that lazy Susan is your best friend.

Floral Base is a brand-new product I was introduced to just before finishing up the book. I was so excited to finally come across a material to replace traditional, harmful floral foam and felt honored to be one of the first florists in the U.S. to get to test it. It is a natural, biodegradable product derived from wool, and so far, it has worked great. I think it will be really useful for making large-scale installations, wedding arbors and chuppahs, and backdrops. It is also practical for arrangements that need to stay in place during transportation. I like that it has a natural brown color, almost like soil. Most stems will go into the block quite easily, even soft stems like ranunculus and tulips! There are a few spots in the blocks where there is a bit of resistance; just find another spot nearby or make a hole with a stick and push your flower in. On pages 44 and 150 you can see how I used it in arrangements.

WHAT I AVOID

Floral foam may be super convenient, but it is also super toxic. Unlike chicken wire or frogs, the foam cannot be used again; it does not decompose; and there is a whole movement among florists to avoid using foam. This is also a very loaded topic among florists, and I really don't like pointing fingers. My advice here is to use your best judgment and research as much as you can about the materials you plan to use.

PUTTING IT ALL TOGETHER

Ikebana-Inspired Arrangement
Using Flower Frog

I have recently fallen in love with making ikebana-inspired arrangements. I often make these at home, with leftover flowers from events and cutoffs from potted plants or my backyard. Once you get in the zone, you will find it so relaxing. In Japan, where the ikebana technique originated in the seventh century, arranging flowers this way is considered a form of meditation.

The ikebana-inspired arrangement is all about color, proportion, balance, symmetry, and asymmetry.

Making an ikebana, or any sparse arrangement, is like painting a picture. You have to be patient and take your time; take a step back every once in a while to see where you are going. It is an organic process, and one of the most important aspects to consider is the way the stem or twig you are going to use grows. Let that inform your decision on where to place it.

In Japan, where the technique originated, arranging flowers this way is considered a form of meditation, and as soon as you start, it is easy to see why.

I can't say enough good things about this ancient approach that is making a big comeback. Not only is it a fun and relatively easy way to arrange flowers, it is also a very cost-effective way to bring some floral beauty to your home.

You can make an ikebana arrangement using as few as three flowers, or you make it full and lush. And when one or two blooms start to fade, just remove them and reposition the rest of the flowers for a brand-new look.

And the best thing with working with a floral frog is that it's super easy to move your flowers around until you are happy.

WHAT YOU NEED

1   low bowl or dish with an approximate 6–8"-wide opening

1   frog (also called Kenzan)

•   Sharp scissors or clippers

•   Floral tack

1   lazy Susan

THE FLOWERS

2   light peach *Anthuriums*

2   light peach ranunculus

1   white ranunculus

1   chocolate lisianthus "Roseanne Brown"

2   brownie tulips

2   small Didiscus, lace flower, plus a few buds

2   orange Pom Pom ranunculus

1   Illex berry stem

2   red leafy twigs

1   stem autumn eucalyptus

Prepare the frog by attaching a good amount of floral tack or putty to the bottom of the frog. For the right amount, I run the floral tack one loop around the frog. Then I roll it my hands to a cord that I attach by pressing it to the bottom of the frog. Last, using what is at hand, for me, it is usually a pair of clippers, I press the frog to the bottom of the vase.

Then I add water.

Now we are ready to start arranging our flowers.

Make sure you have a level and sturdy surface to work on. Set the bowl on your lazy Susan. Ideally, the bowl should also be raised a bit, at chest level, or whatever is comfortable. If your table is low, put the lazy Susan on a bucket or a box.

Here, I started with a couple of big and showy statement flowers that would determine the height of the arrangement.

Then I added the two peach ranunculus, one high and the other really low.

Measure each flower or stem by holding it against the bottom of your vase before cutting.

Next, I added a couple of tiny Queen Anne's lace to get some depth and texture. And then came the two Pom Pom ranunculus.

After that, I added the white ranunculus and the lisianthus on the left side, next the two tulips spilling out to one side, and to the right, I added the berries, twigs, and foliage—and we are all set.

Remember to use your lazy Susan so you can see your arrangement from all sides.

Wall Installation Using Floral Mesh

WHAT YOU NEED

½ roll of gold floral mesh
- Wire cutters
- Biodegradable cable ties or wire
- Floral tack or clear Command hooks
- Lots of branches and flowers—I used dahlias, chrysanthemums, carnations, crown dill, and branches
- Floral water tubes with closures

Making a wall installation like this one is not as hard as it may look or sound, but you need a plan!

First step is to decide on a shape for your installation, like the asymmetrical bow here. If possible, sketch it up with a piece of chalk on the wall. For scale, it is always a good idea to take a few steps back now and then to see where on the wall you have landed.

If you are in the right place, and the shape and size feel right, you can start putting your mesh up by loosely rolling it and fastening it with screws or Command hooks.

Now comes the fun: Adding flowers, twigs, and branches.

As a "rule," I start by spreading the branches somewhat evenly across the floral mesh. This is so you can see the shape, but also so not to damage the flowers that are more delicate and can easily bruise and break.

Many branches will stay in place held by the floral mesh alone, but to secure them, you can use any kind of ties or wire.

When you are ready to add your flowers, fill the tubes with water and secure the lids. Then push the stems into the tubes, and carefully thread them, one by one, through the floral mesh. Hide any visible tubes with foliage. Note: the tubes can be used again if you clean them.

Wide and Loose Arrangement Using Chicken Wire

The idea here is to create a lush and full arrangement but still give each bloom room to show off! These arrangements are pretty and versatile and so much fun to make.

WHAT YOU NEED

1   footed vase with an approximate 6"-wide opening
1   lazy Susan
•   Chicken wire
•   Wire cutter
•   Floral tape
•   Sharp scissors or clippers

THE FLOWERS

For this arrangement I used:

3   cappuccino roses
6   blush peach ranunculus
4   champagne roses
3   stems Majolica spray roses
2   stems Sahara spray roses
6   stems Didiscus, lace flower
4   stems white larkspur
•   Autumn eucalyptus and mixed greens

And this is how I put it together. Always work on a level and sturdy surface. Set the bowl on your lazy Susan. Ideally, the vase should also be raised a bit, almost at chest level, or whatever is comfortable. If your table is low, put the lazy Susan on a bucket or a box.

Using wire cutters, cut a piece of chicken wire the same width and approximately three times the length of the vase opening. Shape the chicken wire into a ball and place it in the vase; secure it by placing floral tape in a cross over the opening. Then add water.

Now it's time to add the flowers. I like to cover the rim with mixed greenery, making sure some drapes over the edge.

If you have a tall bud or two, stick them in now. They will help you determine the height of your arrangement without crowding. Next, I like to add a couple of large blooms down low to create depth. Then I spin my lazy Susan.

Some smaller blooms get tucked in low to create depth. An organized and efficient way to work is to add one type of flower at the time, but I don't always follow this rule.

As I work, I take a step back every once in a while to make sure no blooms are hiding behind others. Scale and proportion are so important in these arrangements. You want a full and lush effect without crowding, texture without mess. Remember, it is totally fine to move your flowers around until you are happy with the result.

As I turn the lazy Susan for a final spin, I add that last bloom that will make all the difference! Knowing when to stop is an art in itself and it takes practice. A rule of thumb is to give every bloom its own space.

Pretty Little Arrangement Using Twigs

Using twigs instead of chicken wire is a fun and organic approach I have come to appreciate. Twigs are easy to work with and cost nothing, and this method allows you to move your flowers around.

This is a pretty small arrangement with just a handful of blooms, but the method works on larger arrangements as well.

Since twigs are less predictable than, say, a flower frog, I would not recommend this method for ikebana-inspired arrangements or when you want to be really precise. Also, the twigs have to be reasonably fresh and flexible and not too dry or stiff.

WHAT YOU NEED

1	bowl with an approximate 6–8"-wide opening
1	lazy Susan
•	Soft twigs
•	Floral tape
•	Sharp scissors or clippers

THE FLOWERS

1	cymbidium orchid stem
3	sweet peas
3	blue nigellas
3	grape hyacinths
2	tweedias
•	Seeded eucalyptus

Always make sure your work surface is sturdy and level. Set your bowl on the lazy Susan. Ideally, the bowl should also be raised a bit, almost at chest level, or whatever is comfortable. If your table is low, put the lazy Susan on a bucket or a box.

Using sharp scissors or clippers, cut the twigs, some three times as long as the width of the vase opening, some twice as long. Push them in to the bowl in no particular order and secure them by placing floral tape in a cross over the opening. Then I add water.

Now we add the flowers.

Start by creating a green base using the seeded eucalyptus. I like the whole rim of the bowl to be covered with a few stems sticking up. Spin your lazy Susan around to check.

Then add the blue nigellas. I always go for a slightly off-center approach to avoid too much symmetry in my arrangements. Continue with the tweedias. You can spread them pretty much all over. They are so tiny and cute and remind me of wildflowers in the spring.

Next comes the main character, the orchid. Place this beauty on either side of the arrangement, depending on the way it bends and shows off its blooms best, but make sure it doesn't stick straight up, or point at three or nine o'clock!

Time to add your sweet peas to the mix. Place them on the opposite side of the orchid for balance. Some of them will want to face up, others down.

Now take a step back and examine your arrangement for balance and texture. Does the orchid look too straight? Can you see all the blooms? Spin the lazy Susan around. Move your flowers around and keep going until it feels right. The last flowers to be added are the small, gestural stems, the grape hyacinths, each one of them cut to a different height.

Again examine the balance with each one you add by using your lazy Susan. Balance is so important in a smaller arrangement with fewer stems—think of balance like a seesaw. Not that each side of the arrangement should match the other, or one should be up and the other down, but rather that one side is offset by an element on the opposite side. If it sounds abstract when you read it, think about it next time you arrange.

140

Midsize Arrangement Using Frog and Chicken Wire

Combining a flower frog with chicken wire allows me to create large- and medium-size arrangements using fewer stems and less greenery. This method is also useful when creating a bit more structured arrangement and when it is really important that each stem stays in place.

WHAT YOU NEED

1 footed vase with an approximate 5–6"-wide opening

1 flower frog

• Floral tack

• Floral tape

1 lazy Susan

• Sharp scissors or clippers

THE FLOWERS

2 jasmine stems

9 ranunculus, soft peach, pink, and orange

3 geranium stems

3 tulips, orange, flexed as shown on page 115

3 light peach carnations

3 *Lindera* benzoin stems

3 mimosa branches

1 blue star fern

• Mixed greenery

First, make sure your work surface is sturdy and level. Set your bowl on the lazy Susan. Ideally, the bowl should also be raised a bit; I like to work at chest level. If your table is too low, put the lazy Susan on a bucket or box.

Prepare the frog by attaching a good amount of floral tack or putty to the bottom of the frog. For the right amount, I run the floral tack one loop around the frog. Then I roll it through my hands to a cord that I attach by pressing it to the bottom of the frog. Last, using what is at hand, usually a pair of scissors, I press the frog, to the bottom of the dry vase.

Then comes the chicken wire. Using wire cutters, cut a piece of chicken wire approximately three times the width of the vase opening. Shape the chicken wire into a ball, place it on the bottom of the vase, and secure it by placing floral tape in a cross over the opening. Then add water.

Even though you don't need a lot of greenery to hold your flowers in place, I like to start with a bit of green anyway. Make sure to remove all leaves that would otherwise be in the water, and then add the stems, one by one while turning the lazy Susan. Try not to get them too symmetrical.

Here, I have added jasmine on the left to set the width of my arrangement and a tall ranunculus to the right to determine height. The pretty geranium leaves and the carnations you can barely see add texture. With the mimosa stems in place, on the right side, and the pretty *Lindera* to the left, you start to get the idea.

Measuring them by holding each stem up to the vase, cut the ranunculus, one by one, and add them all around—don't forget to use your lazy Susan!

Flex the tulips as shown on page **115** and measure them, one by one, before adding them to the right, and you are done!

Bud Vase Arrangements

Filling a few tiny vases with flowers, buds, or greens—or even kitchen herbs—and arranging them in a way that is pleasing to the eye is one of the quickest and least expensive ways of transforming any surface or area.

Amassing a larger group can make quite a statement, or, depending on the origins of the vases, tell a story. When making really small groups, I like to stick with odd numbers, like one, three, or five, but when you cover a bigger area, it really doesn't matter, as long as you have a variety of heights.

This is a great way of repurposing flowers that still look pretty after the rest of a larger arrangement has wilted away, something we do at the studio all the time!

Small vases are also easy to combine with a variety of art objects or collections to create a still life or draw attention to an area that could use a little love.

Arrange a few bud vases on a mantel, in a window, on your dining room table, or anywhere, and watch the space transform.

In this composition (see next page), I have mixed large and small blooms but limited the colors to yellows and blues. Different sizes, heights, and textures always bring interest, but there are really no rules, and almost every little flower likes the company of others. You can use one, two, or three flowers in each little vase, or more if they fit!

When the stems are few, the vases come more into focus and are almost as important as the flowers themselves. Here I have used a mix of clear glass and gray ceramic, but I recommend that you raid your cupboards and stay on the lookout at yard sales and flea markets for cute little bottles, jars, and glasses that can be used as bud vases.

As with all flower arranging, the process of placing the flowers in the right vessel and moving them around until you find the best arrangement is part of the fun!

Collection of Bud Vases in Varying Heights

WHAT I USED:

Arrangements, left to right:

2 blue hyacinths in a low gray vase with an approximate 1"-wide opening; 1 blue larkspur in a tall narrow-mouth glass bottle with an approximate ½"-wide opening; 2 privet berry branches in a low smoky gray glass vase with an approximate ¾"-wide opening; 1 hyacinth, 2 geranium leaves, 3 chinaberry branches in a tall gray ceramic vase with an approximate 1"-wide opening; 1 blue larkspur in a tiny glass bud vase; 2 spider mums, 2 blue gentiana in a gray marble footed bowl with an approximate 3"-wide opening (using a flower frog); 2 light blue larkspur in a glass bud vase; 1 spider mum, 2 chinaberry branches in a narrow-mouthed, short glass vase

Playful Arrangement Using Floral Base

This new product can be used as an alternative to harmful floral foam; it is 100% natural and can be cut to almost any shape and size. In this arrangement, I placed the Floral Base on a low dish, which allowed me to add stems to both the top and sides of the block. This type of arrangement looks really cute on a mantelpiece or rectangular pedestal! You can also make several of these and connect to create a longer arrangement, and it can be used in installations, arbors, chuppahs, and more.

WHAT YOU NEED

1   low dish with an approximate 4–5"-wide opening

1   piece of Floral Base cut to size

•   String or twine

•   Sharp scissors or clippers

THE FLOWERS

8   peach ranunculus in various shades

1   stock bud

4   red spider mums

5   small pom pom dahlias

2   pink dahlias

2   magenta nerines

2   burgundy hanging amaranthus

3   pieces of silk foliage

As always, make sure you have a sturdy area to work on at a height that is comfortable for you.

Start by securing the Floral Base to the dish using string or twine. Then add water—you'll be surprised how thirsty this block is!

When creating playful arrangements like this, I think it is really helpful to determine the size and shape of your arrangement first by choosing a few strategically placed flowers. Here, I used the three dark red spider mums and the two pink dahlias.

For fullness and texture, I added the five pom pom dahlias and, for height, the tall ranunculus.

As a last step, I added the two amaranthus, the silk foliage leaves and the rest of the ranunculus. Since I was using a really low dish, I made sure to cover the base so the twine wouldn't show.

Silk flowers can be reused over and over. We do use them on occasion in our large-scale installations but as a general rule of thumb we only use them mixed with real flowers and at a height where they cannot be touched.

carnations, and poppies; mimosa, golden mustard roses, and lindera benzoin branches. For foliage, I chose geranium leaves, lots of smilax (those long vines), and foraged greenery.

Using watermelon instead of floral foam is a fun method I first tried out at a class I was teaching in sustainable methods for large-scale installations at FlowerSchool LA. Finding alternative methods is crucial in an industry that creates a lot of waste. I had been racking my brain for a long time, trying to think of something that was organic and compostable that could hold flowers in place, and finally thought of this idea.

For this installation, I wanted to create the feeling of an overgrown greenhouse. We attached command hooks in the corner of the window frames then hung watermelon wrapped in chicken wire to the hooks. Thereafter we pushed flowers and vines into the watermelon cages. This also worked well on the floor.

To create additional volume, I incorporated a large arrangement that was prepared at the studio in advance. This is a great trick when you don't have a lot of time to set up. I typically use a planter that is pretty enough to be seen, but at the same time blends with the floor or backdrop. When placing any arrangement on the floor, make sure it is heavy or weighted so it doesn't tip over.

Organic Installation Using Watermelon

WHAT YOU NEED

1   watermelon cut into wedges
·   Chicken wire cut into squares large enough to wrap around your melon wedges
·   Medium gauge florist wire
·   Command hooks
·   Heavy floor pot or urn prepared with chicken wire as shown on page 133

THE FLOWERS

·   Lots of vines, short branches, and flowers—I used various shades of peach amaryllis, ranunculus, spray

RESOURCES

New York Flower Market

West 28th Street, between Sixth and Seventh Avenues, New York, NY

This market is wholesale only, which means that you would have to buy in bulk. But sometimes, if you come late in the day and bring cash, they will sell a smaller quantity. I usually go to Abraflora and I always look for Shadow. He is a true friend and has taught me everything I know about conditioning flowers. Dutch Flower Line is another favorite. If you go to Dutch, ask for Chris or Vinnie—they are true experts!

Chelsea Gardens

444 Van Brunt Street and 87 Havemeyer Street, Brooklyn, NY
chelseagardencenter.com

I often buy potted plants here. Keeping some potted plants around is a great way to make sure you always have flowers and greenery to cut from.

New York City Greenmarkets

grownyc.org

Greenmarkets are wonderful since they bring in growers and sellers from many different areas. Union Square Market, on Broadway and East 17th Street, may be the most famous, but there are wonderful markets in every borough. Go to their website for addresses and market days (or search for markets in your own area).

ALTERNATIVE RETAILERS TO KEEP IN MIND

Corner delis, fruit markets, or bodegas offer flowers at very reasonable prices. Supermarkets have pretty good flowers, both cut and potted.

Blooms by the Box

bloomsbythebox.com

Fifty Flowers

fiftyflowers.com

Bulk Wholesale Flowers

bulkwholesaleflowers.com

STORES, STUDIOS, AND ONLINE VENDORS

The Gallery at 200 Lex

nydc.com/antiques/

Huge upscale art and antiques gallery with over fifty vendors.

Frances Palmer

francespalmerpottery.com

Connecticut-based potter and one of the very best. Vases, pots, and everything for your tablescape; functional art, so special and pretty!

Bloomist

bloomist.com

Great online vendor with some really nice and unusual pieces, many made here in the United States. It's a great place to find interesting objects for your still life or tablescape.

WrenLab Ceramics

wrenlabceramics.com

Wheel-thrown porcelain vases made by Erin Banta Wilford, an Italian-born, Arizona-trained, and Brooklyn-based artist. I love and want everything she makes!

28A Clay

28aclay.com

This is a fairly new studio in the Catskills, run by Meredith and Harry Kunhardt, two self-taught potters. Cool and rustic vases and bowls made from locally sourced clay.

abc carpet & home

888 Broadway, New York, NY
abchome.com

Like a giant toy store where you can find everything for your flowers and the rest of your home; large online selection of vases as well.

Wilcoxson Brooklyn Ceramics

67 West Street, Greenpoint, Brooklyn, NY
wilcoxsonbrooklynceramics.com

Modern and really cool ceramic bowls, bottles, and cups that can be used as vases. Online store as well.

Horseman Antiques

351 Atlantic Avenue, Brooklyn, NY
horsemanantiques.net

You can find some really special pieces here. Sometimes it pays to spend a little more on an urn or vase that you will love forever.

Holler & Squall
304 Henry Street, Brooklyn, NY
hollerandsquall.com

City Foundry Showroom
369 Atlantic Avenue, Brooklyn, NY
cityfoundry.com
A pioneer of the Brooklyn design movement, this store is a must for everyone interested in design and the Brooklyn brand. You will find some totally unique pieces here.

Sterling Place
363 Atlantic Avenue, Brooklyn, NY
sterlingplace.com
Eclectic and unusual objects mixed with reasonably priced pitchers, glasses, and vases.

Brooklyn Flea
80 Pearl Street, Brooklyn, NY and 29 West 25th Street, New York, NY
brooklynflea.com
Open every weekend during the summer, these markets are a must for the collector. In the winter, the market moves to Industry City in Sunset Park.

Yesterday's News
428 Court Street, Brooklyn, NY
yesterdaysnews.biz
With most of its inventory out on the sidewalk, this store feels like a really good yard sale.

Salvation Army
salvationarmyusa.org
This could be a hit or miss, but sometimes you find a true bargain, and when you do, you help someone else. Go to their website for the thrift store nearest you.

Etsy
etsy.com
I love Etsy! You can find almost anything here, and usually at pretty good prices!

West Elm
westelm.com

Anthropologie
anthropologie.com

The Container Store
containerstore.com
They have some really cute jars and bottles here that I have used for events. I also use their plastic containers to line my wooden crates. Super cheap!

Terrain
shopterrain.com
They offer a large selection of urns and vases, some reasonable, others pretty expensive.

CB2
cb2.com

H&M Home
hm.com

Zara Home
zarahome.com

Sounds
157 Seventh Avenue, Brooklyn, NY
shopsounds.nyc
This is a really fun store for colorful vases and décor items where you can grab a cup of coffee while you shop.

Wanderlustre
262 Court Street, Brooklyn, NY
wanderlustre.com

A truly eclectic assortment of objects and table décor awaits you here. It's such a fun place to roam around, and I have found some really nice brass bowls here.

Painted Swan
407 Court Street, Brooklyn, NY
paintedswan.com
This is such a pretty store where almost everything is white and painted in Annie Sloan chalk paint. They have a large collection of ironstone pottery that goes beautifully with my lush flower arrangements.

Nicholas Newcomb
nicholasnewcomb.com
Beautiful one-of-a-kind pieces I use when I want to do something really special for a client or a friend.

TOOLS & SUPPLIES

Jamali Floral & Garden Supplies
jamaligarden.com
Everything for the florist: clippers, tape, wire, chicken wire, spray bottles, knives, pots, vases—everything!

Ace Hardware, Lowe's, and Home Depot
Shopping at your hardware store is often the least expensive way to go for chicken wire, hardware, paint, masking tape, and tools.

Michaels
michaels.com
Great place for basic bottles, vases, and containers you can use as they are, or transform with paint, which they also sell.

Blick Art Materials
dickblick.com
This is my go-to place for more specialized art supplies, like high-quality paintbrushes.

FLOWER SCHOOLS

US
FlowerSchool New York
213 West 14th Street, New York, NY
flowerschoolny.com
FlowerSchool New York is the most prestigious school for floral arts and design on the East Coast, providing a vast array of floral design classes from beginner to advanced certification. The school also brings in the most sought-after designers from all over the world to teach their uniquely comprehensive programs.

CANADA
Canadian Institute of Floral Design Inc.
2794A Lakeshore Boulevard West
Toronto, ON M8V 1H5
cifd.ca
CIFD, has been in business since 1988. Their Professional Floral Design Program prepares students for a career in the floral industry through 105 hours of hands-on training, over a three-week session.

UK
London Flower School
16–20 Wharfdale Road, London, N1 9RY, UK
londonflowerschool.com
Founded by Wagner Kreusch and Helen Dyson, London Flower School is known to push boundaries in floristry, challenge the traditional notions of the discipline, and bring dynamic new concepts to life. They run floristry courses for both new and experienced florists and encourage students to develop their own creative vision and find inspiration beyond the world of flowers.

NETHERLANDS
Boerma Instituut International Floral Design School Holland
Legmeerdijk 227, 1432KA Aalsmeer, Holland
boerma.com
Now in their fortieth year of operation, the Boerma Instituut offers classes for all levels, and all over the world! Their vision is to design and create flower arrangements while sharing their family's love of flowers. Classes range from professional floristry courses, master classes, hobby courses, and event design courses.

RUSSIA
Araik Galstyan Moscow School
araikgalstyan.com/eng/
Arayik Galstyan Moscow International Floral Design School offers a master-level program designed for current and future professionals. The school is open to students of all levels, from beginner to professional, interested in improving their skills and becoming more competitive in the market.

AUSTRALIA
Pearsons School of Floristry
50 Oxford Street, Darlinghurst NSW 2010, Australia
pearsonsschool.com.au
At Pearsons, they aim to share the passion and knowledge developed over fifty years in the industry in an innovative and creative environment. Led by a team of talented teachers, the programs are design to deliver an inspiring learning experience.

ASIA
Mami Flower Design School, Tokyo
2–11–6 Sanno, Ota-ku, Tokyo 143-0023, Japan
mamifds.co.jp
Founded in the sixties, this Tokyo-based organization has over three hundred schools throughout Japan and overseas. They offer classes in traditional Japanese techniques as well as contemporary styles.

The H.K. Academy of Flower Arrangement
15/F, Hennessy Plaza, 164 Hennessy Road, Wanchai, Hong Kong
hkafa.com.hk/en
The H.K. Academy of Flower Arrangement was founded in 1989 and is the first flower school in Hong Kong to introduce international floral designs. The academy adheres to a modern teaching philosophy, ensuring that students can integrate floral creation elements into interior design and current international trends. The school offers a wide variety of courses and attracts sought-after teachers from all over the world.

ACKNOWLEDGMENTS

I am so grateful to all of the collaborators who participated and helped bring this book to life.

First and foremost, I want to thank my Stella, the most inspiring kid on this planet. You choose to see the world with compassion and great interest, and I learn so much from you every day.

And thank you to Maj, my mother, for making flowers part of my life from a very early age through the lovely gardens you kept, big or small, wherever we lived in the world.

Then of course, the tastemakers, who are the heart and soul of this book. Thank you for sharing your spaces with me and my team, thank you for being so generous with your time, even when we had to pause and restart throughout a pandemic! Thank you for supplying an endless amount of inspiration.

Thank you, Renée Lundholm, for seeing my potential and thinking I should work with flowers before I did.

Thanks to Eva, who came up with the idea for my first book. I am so glad you joined me for the second one.

Thanks so much to Meredith Clark at Abrams, for suggesting that we write another book! It has been such a pleasure!

Thanks to Ashley, so organized, smart, and always with a positive outlook. You make my life so much easier and without you, none of this would be possible. And of course the entire team at Tin Can Studios, and those who assisted so perfectly in creating some of the arrangements for this book: Taj Robinson, Shelby Simpson, Kristen Usui, Rachel Sunae, Nikki Pettus, Katherine Carothers, Michelle Hannah, Irina Motuz, Vicki Zhuk, Anna Lundquist, and Ellen Irhee. Your dedication and talent is limitless, I love you guys like family.

Dana Gallagher, you sure do understand how to create the best compositions.

Dane Tashima, your eye for line, form, and detail is impeccable.

Thank you, Judy Linden, for your advice and kind support.

Thank you to so many teachers and friends who have supported me throughout this process: Gabriele Wilson, William van Roden, Nicky Balisteri.

Thank you, Brittney Summers and Molly Findlay, for so generously allowing us to invade your homes with flowers during a time where we had to socially distance.

Thanks to Chris Harkness, for suggesting we use your beautiful space and for inspiring me through food as well as introducing us to Wells Stellberger at 99 Scott.

And thanks to 99 Scott for lending us your beautiful space, especially on the day that events were "put on pause" and we had to improvise.

Many thanks to Ollcore Studio, Evergreen Antiques, Lawton Mull, Carswell Rush Berlin Antiques, Modern Antiquarian, Clinton Howell Antiques, Milord Antiques, Hyde Park Antiques, Ltd., and Elizabeth Pash Interiors & Antiques, the kind dealers who lent us furniture, vases, mirrors, and art. They were all spectacular. And thank you to The Gallery at 200 Lex for letting Michael build his dream space.

Every successful florist must have "a guy" at their local flower market. I have at least one at each wholesale store: Chris, Vinnie, Edgar, Jordy, and Cas at Dutch Flower Line. Nic, Roland, Troy at J Rose, Fabian, Rich and Edwin at G Page, Persuad at 28 St Wholesalers, David at Rallis, Tom at Caribbean Cuts, Kenny at Holiday, Gus at U.S. Evergreens, all the guys at Associated. And last, but certainly not least, my best friend Shadow at AbraFlora, who has taught me everything I know about flowers.

Thanks to my clients who continue to inspire and send me the most exciting projects, and a special thanks to those of you who supported Tin Can Studios throughout the pandemic by ordering our Bloom Boxes.

I am so grateful,
Ingrid Carozzi

ARTISAN CREDITS

I'd like to especially say thank you to the following for their kind donations of the vases used throughout this book.

Vases were provided by:

Nicholas Newcomb, page 10
West Elm, page 16
 Huset, page 34
Bloomist, page 36
Kenzan Kiev, page 45
Painted Swan, pages 52–53
Painted Swan, page 54
Frances Palmer, page 55
Melanie Abrantes, page 69
Nicholas Newcomb, page 70

Les Guimards, page 71
Melanie Abrantes and Matagalan
    Plantae, pages 92–93
Nicholas Newcomb, page 116
WrenLab Ceramics, Nicholas
    Newcomb, West Elm, and 28A
    Clay and Private, pages 118–119
Jessica Hahn, WanderLustre, Etsy,
    Terrain, and Painted Swan, pages
    120–121

Editor: Meredith A. Clark
Managing Editor: Glenn Ramirez
Designer: Darilyn Lowe Carnes
Production Manager: Kathleen Gaffney

Library of Congress Control Number: 2021932495

ISBN: 978-1-4197-4618-5
eISBN: 978-1-68335-953-1

Printed and bound in China
10 9 8 7 6 5 4 3 2 1

Abrams books are available at special discounts when purchased in quantity
for premiums and promotions as well as fundraising or educational use.
Special editions can also be created to specification. For details, contact
specialsales@abramsbooks.com or the address below.

Abrams® is a registered trademark of Harry N. Abrams, Inc.

ABRAMS The Art of Books
195 Broadway, New York, NY 10007
abramsbooks.com